AF866572

Markets Are Systems, Not Signals

Markets Are Systems, Not Signals

Liquidity, Positioning, Volatility, Trend—and Why No One Perspective Is Enough

Saeed Mohammad

WALLSTREETDELTA INSTITUTE

Copyright © 2026 Saeed Mohammad
All rights reserved.
This book is a derivative work based on *Foundations of Market Systems Science*, Volume I, by the same author. Where the two differ in meaning, the scholarly volume governs.
Nothing in this book is investment advice, a recommendation to buy or sell any security or instrument, or a statement that any framework, method, or observation will improve investment results. No such claim is made, and no evidence establishing one is offered. Readers responsible for financial decisions remain responsible for them.

Published by WallStreetDelta Institute

ISBN 979-8-9975240-1-2 (paperback)

First Edition

About This Edition

A note on this edition

This is a retail edition. It is derived from *Foundations of Market Systems Science*, Volume I, a scholarly work of roughly twice this length that carries the full argument, the complete measurement and research standards, the principle register, the appendices, and the bibliography.

This edition may simplify, compress, reorganize, and add examples. It does not introduce different definitions. Where a term is used here, it means what it means in the scholarly volume. Where a distinction is drawn here, it is drawn there. Readers who want the full treatment — including the research method, model governance, and the standards by which the framework should be evaluated and, where necessary, revised — should read Volume I.

Several things in the scholarly volume are deliberately not reproduced here: research protocols, measurement specifications, model documentation standards, and the governance apparatus that supports professional use. Their absence is a choice about audience, not a claim that they do not matter.

On what is original here, and what is not

Almost none of the underlying material is new, and the book says so repeatedly because it is true.

Liquidity, positioning, volatility, and trend are long-established subjects with extensive research literatures. So are measurement theory, statistical inference, causal reasoning, decision theory, model risk management, reproducible research, and the philosophy of science that the second chapter rests on. The framework described here does not claim to have originated the distinction between observation and theory, provisional knowledge, hypothesis testing, model uncertainty, measurement validity, Bayesian updating, replication, or decision analysis. Each is a mature field with its own literature and its own continuing disagreements.

What is proposed is organization: the arrangement of established disciplines into one architecture for reasoning about markets, beginning with observation rather than with an indicator, and preserving the path from measurement to evidence to assessment to judgment to decision.

The scholarly volume documents this attribution chapter by chapter. This edition states it once, here, and returns to it in the conclusion.

Who this book is for

Anyone who follows markets closely enough to have been misled by confident explanations of them.

It assumes you know what a share, a bond, an option, and a futures contract are. It does not assume any mathematics, and it contains none. It does not assume you trade, and it will not help you trade — that is not modesty, and the reason is worked out in the final chapter.

What it offers is a way of telling the difference between a claim about markets that is supported and one that merely sounds supported. That turns out to be a more durable skill than any particular method of analysis, because methods decay and the ability to evaluate them does not.

How to read it

The chapters build. Chapter 2 establishes vocabulary the rest of the book uses constantly, and skipping it will make Chapters 8 through 11 harder than they need to be.

The four domain chapters — liquidity, positioning, volatility, and trend — can be read in any order, but all four should be read before Chapter 8, which is where they stop being four separate subjects.

The conclusion can be read first. It is a set of tests for judging claims about markets, and some readers will want to know what the book is building toward before building it.

Contents

PART ONE

Foundations

Chapters 1–2

> Every discipline begins not with answers but with a disciplined way of asking questions.

Before anything useful can be said about a particular market, two things have to be settled: what kind of thing a market is, and how anyone comes to know anything about it.

Neither is obvious. Markets are usually described as if they were mechanisms that respond to inputs — news arrives, prices adjust. That description is not wrong so much as incomplete, and the part it leaves out turns out to be the part that explains why identical news produces different outcomes.

The second question is less often asked at all. Market data arrive with an authority that other kinds of evidence have to earn: precise, timestamped, and apparently direct. Most of that authority is borrowed. Between a market event and a claim about it sit half a dozen transformations, each of which selects something and discards something else.

These two chapters do that groundwork. The first is about what markets are. The second is about the difference between what you have observed, what you have measured, what you have inferred, and what you have assumed — and it introduces the vocabulary that the rest of the book uses constantly.

CHAPTER ONE

Markets Are Systems, Not Signals

Two markets, one announcement

Imagine the same piece of news arriving in two different markets on the same afternoon. A policy decision, moderately unfavorable to risk assets. Not a shock. Not a surprise anyone will still be discussing in a month.

In the first market, prices slip. Within twenty minutes buyers appear, the decline stalls, and by the close the move looks ordinary. Someone writes that the market "took it in stride."

In the second market, the same announcement produces a decline three times as large. Selling accelerates rather than fading. Prices move further on smaller and smaller trades. By late afternoon the commentary has moved from the policy decision to the word "fragile," and by evening someone is explaining that investors were frightened.

The information was identical. The reaction was not.

There is a comfortable explanation for this, and it is wrong. The comfortable explanation is that the second market had worse news, or worse investors, or worse luck. The more useful explanation is that the two markets were arranged differently before the announcement arrived.

In the first, the capacity to absorb selling was deep. Exposure was spread across many participants with different time horizons and different obligations. Few of them were close to a limit that would force them to act. In the second, that same capacity was thin. Exposure was concentrated, financed with borrowed money, and clustered near thresholds where a modest decline compels a sale whether or not anyone has changed their mind about anything.

The announcement started the move in both markets. It did not determine the size of the move in either. What determined the size was everything that was already true before the announcement arrived.

That is the central claim of this book, and everything else in it is an attempt to make the claim precise: **what happens in a market depends less on the event than on the system the event lands in.**

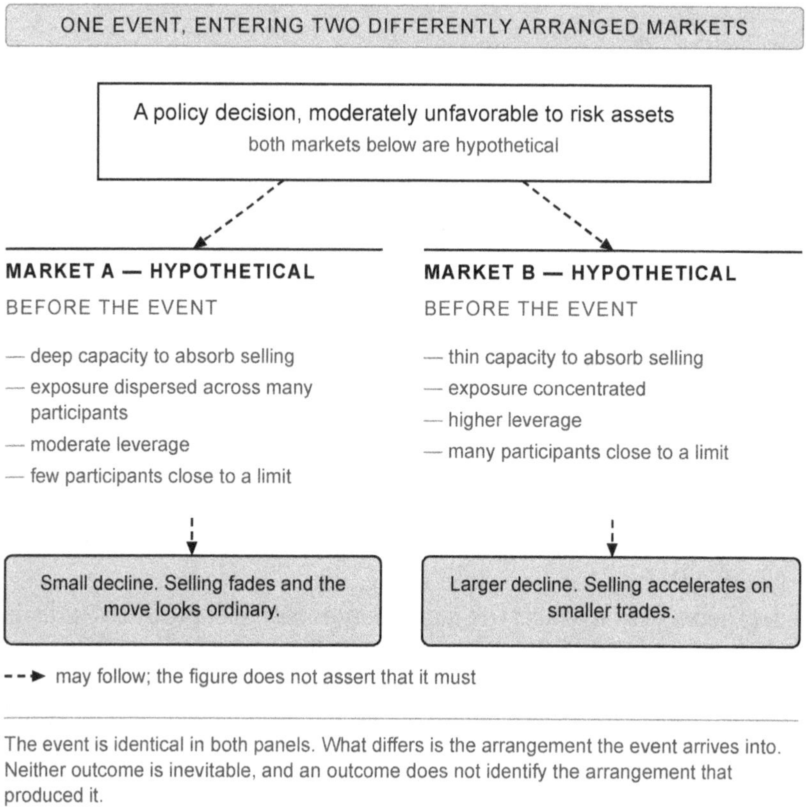

Figure 1. One event, two differently arranged markets, two outcomes. Both markets are hypothetical.

The problem with reading markets one number at a time

Most market commentary works in a single dimension. A number moves, and the number is assigned a meaning. Volatility rose, so investors are frightened. Volume was heavy, so conviction was strong. The index closed above a moving average, so the trend is intact. Open interest increased, so somebody is positioning for something.

Each of these statements has the shape of an explanation without the substance of one. Each takes one measurement, detaches it from the conditions that give it meaning, and converts it into a conclusion about the whole market.

The alternative is not more numbers. Adding indicators to a screen that already has too many produces a different failure: a wall of information that resists interpretation, where every position can be supported by selecting a favorable subset. Accumulation and reduction fail in opposite directions, and both fail.

What is missing in each case is structure. Not more observations, but a disciplined way of relating observations to one another, and of knowing what any one of them can and cannot establish on its own.

That is what this book is about. It is not a method for reading markets faster. It is a method for being clear about what you actually know.

What makes something a system

The word gets used loosely, so it is worth being precise. Across engineering, biology, ecology, and physics, a system is generally understood as a collection of interacting components whose relationships produce behavior that cannot be fully understood by examining the components separately.

The defining feature is interaction, not size.

A pile of sand contains an enormous number of grains, and the grains barely interact. Remove one and the pile is unchanged. Describe the pile and you have described the grains.

An ecosystem also contains many components, but its components act on one another continuously. Remove one species and predator–prey relationships shift, nutrient cycles change, populations rearrange. Describing the organisms individually does not describe the ecosystem.

Financial markets are the second kind of thing. A price is not a property that an asset possesses. It emerges from the continual interaction of buyers, sellers, institutions, regulations, technologies, information, and expectations. Understanding a market therefore requires studying both its components and the relationships among them.

The components are not mysterious. **Participants** with different objectives: individuals, pension funds, corporate treasurers, market makers, index funds, algorithmic systems. **Information**, which affects markets only after it has been interpreted by someone. **Mechanisms** through which buyers and sellers actually meet: exchanges, matching engines, clearing, settlement. **Incentives**, which differ by participant and explain why the same price looks attractive to one and unacceptable to another. And **constraints**: capital, leverage, regulation, mandates, risk limits, available time. Constraints will turn out to matter as much as objectives, and possibly more, because a participant who wants to hold and is required to sell will sell.

Behavior comes from interaction

No single participant determines a market. No single economic report determines it. No single indicator determines it. What is observable is the aggregate result of many simultaneous processes, most of them invisible.

Consider a market where institutional buying is increasing while economic expectations are deteriorating. At the same time, price variability is falling, the exposures of options dealers are shifting, and the available liquidity is concentrating near a small number of price levels.

None of those observations describes the market. Any one of them, presented alone, would support a confident and probably wrong story. Together they may describe a coherent arrangement of conditions that could not have been inferred from any of them individually.

This is why the emphasis throughout this book falls on relationships among observations rather than on the observations themselves.

Four properties worth knowing by name

Markets belong to a broader class of systems that scientists call *complex adaptive systems*. Definitions vary, but four properties appear consistently and each of them will do real work later in this book.

Emergence. Some market phenomena exist only at the level of the whole. Liquidity is not a property of any one participant. Neither is momentum, nor the tendency of volatile periods to cluster together. These arise from collective behavior and cannot be located in any individual actor.

Adaptation. Participants change. Strategies are tested, copied, crowded, and abandoned. Risk tolerances shift. Technology moves. Regulation responds to failure. A relationship that held reliably for a decade may weaken precisely because enough people noticed it. This is why market knowledge decays in a way that knowledge of, say, thermodynamics does not.

Feedback. Actions change the environment, and the changed environment influences later actions. A price decline may attract buyers who consider the asset cheaper, which opposes the move. The same decline may trigger margin calls, stop orders, and hedging that reinforces it. The important point is that the *same mechanism* can stabilize one market and destabilize another, depending on the arrangement it operates in. Feedback is not inherently a spiral.

Nonlinearity. Response is not proportional to input. A small update may produce almost nothing when capacity is deep, exposure is balanced, and variability is contained. The identical update may produce a large move when capacity is thin, borrowing is high, exposure is concentrated, and participants sit near limits. This is the property that made our two markets behave differently, and it is why a modest catalyst can precede a large adjustment without anything about the catalyst being remarkable.

To these four it is worth adding a fifth, which is less often named and matters constantly.

Path dependence. Two markets can show similar prices and similar variability while having arrived there by different routes, and the route influences what happens next. A gradual advance supported by broad participation leaves behind a different arrangement of exposures than a rapid rebound driven by traders closing losing short positions, even if both end at the same index level. Portfolios carry positions accumulated earlier. Participants remember the last time this happened. Risk controls exist because something once went wrong. The present is not fully described by a snapshot.

Systems thinking does not replace analysis

There is a version of systems thinking that becomes an excuse for vagueness: everything is connected, therefore nothing can be said. That is not the position here.

Scientific work alternates between two complementary approaches. **Reductionism** studies components in isolation and has produced most of what is reliably known about market microstructure, option pricing, and portfolio behavior. **Systems thinking** studies the relationships among components. Neither is sufficient alone. Individual measurements remain essential; understanding emerges when those measurements are integrated into a broader picture of an evolving market.

The shift is in the question. Instead of asking *what does this indicator mean*, the question becomes *what does this observation contribute to my understanding of this market right now*. Individual measurements stop being conclusions and become evidence. Evidence contributes to understanding. Understanding supports explanation. Explanation informs judgment. That sequence is the architecture of this book, and Chapter 2 takes it apart carefully.

It is also worth saying what the systems view costs. Systems models can oversimplify. Relationships change through time. Many interactions are not observable at all. Emergent behavior is genuinely hard to anticipate. Viewing markets as systems does not eliminate uncertainty and does not guarantee explanation. It provides an organizing framework within which observations can be interpreted more coherently, and that is a smaller claim than it may sound, and an honest one.

Nine things that stay true

Markets change continuously. Instruments are created and retired. Venues evolve. Regulations shift. Technology alters the speed, visibility, and cost of trading. Beneath that variation, a small number of propositions remain useful across instruments, decades, and technologies. They are worth stating plainly, because they are the boundaries within which any explanation of market behavior has to fit.

Markets exist to facilitate exchange. Shares transfer a claim on a company. Bonds transfer capital for promised payments. Futures reallocate exposure to a future price. Options redistribute uneven risk. A market is not a price series with a ticker attached; it is a mechanism through which participants transfer ownership, funding, and risk. Prices are an important output of that mechanism, not the mechanism itself.

Participants differ. A transaction does not require the buyer and seller to agree about anything except the terms. A long-term investor may buy because future cash flows look attractive. A dealer may sell the same instrument to manage inventory. A corporation may transact to hedge an operating exposure. An index fund may trade because a rule says so. Each can act at the same price for entirely different reasons. This is why "the market thinks" is almost always a category error: market activity aggregates unlike decisions made for unlike reasons.

Prices emerge from interaction. There is no independent object called true value that the market is discovering. Price emerges from a process in which participants submit, revise, accept, and withdraw terms. That process is shaped by the mechanism: an auction, a dealer market, a limit-order book, and a bilateral negotiation do not reconcile intentions in the same way. Prices contain information. They do not contain all information, and they do not reveal hidden liquidity, unexpressed demand, latent constraints, or what anyone will do next.

Behavior is constrained. An investor may prefer to hold and still sell to meet redemptions. A dealer may find a position attractive and still reduce it because an inventory limit binds. Constraints convert opinions into actions that appear inconsistent with those opinions, and forced liquidation is the clearest case: a participant may sell not because their view of value changed but because their financing did.

Participants adapt. A profitable relationship attracts capital, which reduces the opportunity, shifts its timing, or creates a new vulnerability. Market makers adjust pricing when order flow changes. Institutions redesign hedges after a stress event. Adaptation happens at very different speeds: milliseconds for algorithms, months for allocators, years for institutions and regulation. Those overlapping clocks are one reason markets are hard.

Actions feed back. Discussed above, and worth restating as a boundary: an explanation that treats a market's response as independent of the market's own subsequent reaction is incomplete.

Response is nonlinear. Also discussed above. As a boundary: an explanation that expects proportionality across regimes will be wrong exactly when it matters.

Condition is multidimensional. Price alone cannot reveal whether a move occurred through deep capacity or a thin one. Volume alone cannot reveal execution capacity. Variability alone cannot distinguish orderly repricing from unstable stress. Exposure alone cannot determine whether concentration will unwind or sit inert. A trend can be strong while the capacity to trade deteriorates. Variability can be low while exposure concentrates. This proposition is the one that organizes the middle of this book.

Uncertainty is permanent. Market observers work with incomplete, delayed, transformed, and model-dependent information. Intentions are not visible. Future decisions have not been made. Relationships change as participants adapt. Better data reduces some uncertainty and cannot remove the openness of an adaptive system populated by people making choices. This is not an excuse for vague analysis. It is a higher standard: state what is known, what is inferred, what remains uncertain, and what evidence would change the assessment.

These are boundaries, not predictions

It matters what kind of statement those nine are. They are not laws of price movement. Knowing that participants are heterogeneous does not reveal which group will dominate tomorrow. Knowing that feedback exists does not establish whether it will stabilize or amplify. Knowing that markets are nonlinear does not locate the threshold.

Scientific language should reflect the strength of the underlying claim, and several kinds of claim get confused in market writing. A **principle** is a broad proposition that organizes understanding across contexts. A **tendency** occurs frequently but not invariably: thin liquidity tends to increase price sensitivity to order imbalance. A **recurring mechanism** repeatedly contributes to outcomes without producing the same result every time: leveraged losses can trigger forced selling through margin constraints. An **empirical regularity** is a relationship repeatedly observed under stated conditions, and it can weaken when institutions or behavior change. A **law** is an exceptionally strong, clearly scoped, repeatedly validated relationship, and the word should be used very sparingly about adaptive systems full of people who read.

The nine propositions above are principles in that sense. Their usefulness is as questions imposed on an explanation. Does this account identify what was actually being exchanged? Does it account for participants having different objectives and different constraints? Does it consider adaptation and feedback? Is the relationship scoped to a horizon and a market structure? Does the conclusion rest on more than one dimension, and does it acknowledge what remains unknown?

An explanation that survives those questions can still be wrong. Scientific quality does not guarantee a correct forecast. What it does is make the reasoning traceable, limit overstatement, and make errors informative when outcomes differ from expectations. None of these propositions should be converted into a trading instruction, and this book will not convert them.

What this book is trying to do

The field this book draws on has a name: Market Systems Science. It is the interdisciplinary study of financial markets as evolving complex adaptive systems, through systematic observation, measurement, evaluation of evidence, analysis of how conditions are arranged, investigation of how those arrangements change, and support for decisions.

That definition contains four commitments worth separating.

Markets are treated as **systems**, so behavior is understood as emerging from interaction rather than from isolated variables. They are treated as **adaptive**, so participants are expected to change as information, incentives, and outcomes change. They are treated as **evolving** rather than static, so the market's condition is understood as moving continuously through arrangements and changes rather than sitting in permanent equilibrium. And the discipline begins with **systematic observation** rather than with opinion.

The fourth commitment is the one that shapes the last part of this book: understanding a market and deciding what to do are related but genuinely different activities. Investigation improves understanding. What any particular participant should do with that understanding depends on their objectives, obligations, constraints, and capacity to absorb loss. Those are not properties of the market. They are properties of the participant.

It is equally important to be clear about what falls outside. Market Systems Science does not seek to identify guaranteed strategies, eliminate uncertainty, predict markets with certainty, or replace economics, finance, or statistics. It offers a structured way for those disciplines to contribute to a clearer understanding of how markets behave. If you are looking for a system that tells you what to buy, this is not that, and the reason is not modesty. It is that the framework's own principles rule it out.

How the rest of the book is organized

Three questions run through everything that follows.

How do we know what we know about markets? That is the subject of Chapter 2, which builds the ladder connecting a recorded observation to a defensible conclusion, and shows where each rung can break.

What is the market doing, and how is it arranged? That is Part II. Chapter 3 introduces four perspectives on a market — its capacity to trade, the exposure still sitting on participants' books, the variability of its prices, and the persistence of its direction. Chapters 4 through 7 take each in turn. Chapter 8 puts them back together, which is where the systems argument of this first chapter finally does concrete work.

How does it change, and what should that mean for a decision? Part III asks how an arrangement of conditions gets summarized, and how you tell a genuine change from ordinary movement. Part IV asks what any of this means for someone who has to act under uncertainty, and answers, carefully, that it depends on who is asking.

Those three questions correspond to three pillars that give the field its shape: Market Understanding, Market Evolution, and Market Judgment. They are separated deliberately, because they answer different questions and because collapsing them is the most common way market reasoning goes wrong.

Takeaway

The same news produces different outcomes in different markets, and the difference lives in the market rather than in the news. That is not a metaphor. It is a claim about how markets work, and it has consequences: a single measurement cannot describe a market, a catalyst does not explain the size of a response, and an explanation that ignores constraints, feedback, adaptation, and history is incomplete even when it turns out to be right.

None of this makes markets predictable. It makes them describable with more discipline than a single number allows. The next chapter is about what that discipline actually requires, starting with the most underrated question in market analysis: how do you know that what you think you know is true?

CHAPTER TWO

How We Know What We Know About Markets

A sentence that sounds like knowledge

Here is a sentence of the kind that appears every trading day, in newsletters, on broadcasts, and in the notes of serious professionals:

> The index fell 1.8% as investors, frightened by weakening liquidity, rushed to hedge.

It is fluent, causal, and complete. It has a fact, a mechanism, a motive, and a consequence. It is also five different claims wearing one coat, and they are not equally supported.

That the index fell 1.8% is a record: a specific source reported a specific value over a specific interval. That liquidity weakened is a measurement question, and the answer depends entirely on what was measured, over what horizon, against which baseline. That investors were frightened is a claim about mental states that no market data can establish. That the fear caused the hedging is a causal claim requiring evidence the sentence does not contain. And that the hedging caused the decline reverses the order in which any of it was observed.

Pull those apart and the sentence loses most of its authority. That is the point. This chapter is about how to pull them apart, and about what is left when you do — which is usually less than the sentence claimed and more useful than nothing.

The ladder

Every claim about a market sits somewhere on a ladder that runs from what happened to what someone did about it. The rungs are worth naming, because almost every failure in market reasoning is a rung being skipped or two rungs being treated as one.

The market phenomenon is the thing itself. A transaction occurs. A quotation is posted or withdrawn. Someone holds an exposure that nobody outside their firm can see. This exists whether or not anyone records it.

A recorded observation is what an identified source reported about that activity, under a specific timestamp and format. An exchange reports a trade. A vendor normalizes, consolidates, corrects, or enriches that record. A database stores it with further transformation. What arrives is useful and is not the same thing as direct access to the market.

A measurement is a controlled representation built from those records according to a defined method, for a stated purpose. A closing price is a record; a daily return calculated from successive closing prices is a measurement. Bid and ask quotations are records; their difference is a spread measurement. A sequence of transaction prices is a record; realized volatility calculated from it is a measurement.

Evidence is a measurement placed in relation to a question. This is the rung readers most often skip, and it deserves its own section below.

Inference extends beyond what was measured. If spreads widen, depth falls, and the price moves further per unit traded, an analyst may infer that trading conditions are becoming less resilient. Nobody observed resilience. It was inferred from the combination and the reasoning connecting the parts.

Interpretation organizes evidence and inference into meaning: the market looks increasingly sensitive to adjustment, or increasingly concentrated.

Assessment synthesizes evidence, alternative explanations, contradictions, gaps, and confidence into a qualified view. An assessment might conclude that short-horizon stress is developing while evidence of broader dysfunction remains incomplete.

Judgment forms a conclusion for a stated purpose. **Decision** selects among alternatives under objectives and constraints. **Action** implements the selection. **Outcome and review** feed back into the whole chain, which is why this is a loop rather than a pipeline. Analysts move backward all the time: when evidence is challenged, when a measurement turns out to be wrong, when a model fails, when a result raises a question nobody had asked.

The last three rungs belong to Chapter 11, because they are not properties of the market at all. They are properties of the person acting.

The value of the ladder is not that reasoning becomes mechanical. It is that the boundaries stay visible, so a claim can be traced back to what actually supports it.

What a record can establish

A record answers a narrow question: what did an identified source report?

That narrowness is a feature. "The identified exchange reported this trade at this price and time" is a defensible statement. It does not establish who was on the other side, what they intended, what liquidity was available but not displayed, or what the trade meant.

The narrowness also has an edge to it. Market records are rarely untouched. A trade message may already carry venue-specific conditions, corrections, sequencing rules, instrument mappings, and timestamp conventions applied by exchanges, vendors, consolidators, and software before anyone looked at it. Values may be delayed, stale, corrected, cancelled, missing, or transformed. The phrase "raw data" should be used with suspicion. A record's processing history is part of its meaning.

What a measurement is, and what it is not

A measurement depends on definitions, sampling, horizons, transformations, units, baselines, and assumptions. Two competent analysts can calculate different but entirely defensible numbers from the same underlying records because they chose different windows or different methods. This is not a scandal; it is what measurement is.

The important discipline is that a measurement represents an aspect of a phenomenon without being that phenomenon. Four cases are worth memorizing, because each of them is routinely collapsed in public commentary:

- A **bid-ask spread** represents one dimension of visible trading friction. It is not liquidity.
- **Open interest** represents outstanding contracts. It is not positioning, and it does not reveal who holds which side or whether the exposure is offset somewhere else.
- A **moving average** summarizes prior prices. It is not a trend, and it is certainly not a mechanism.
- **Implied volatility** is inferred from option prices through a pricing model. It is not uncertainty.

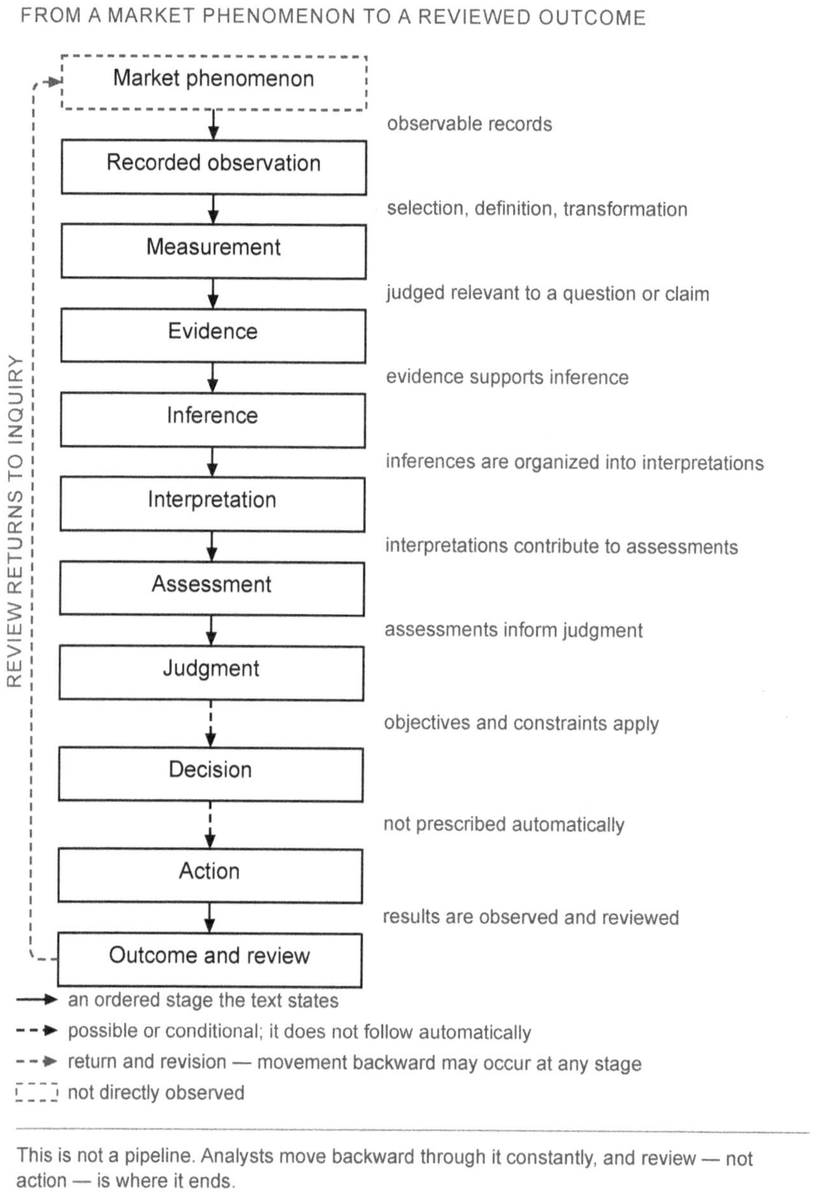

Figure 2. From a market phenomenon to a reviewed outcome, and back. The chain is iterative, not a pipeline.

That last one deserves a moment now and a full treatment in Chapter 6. An option premium is observed. Implied volatility is generally obtained by solving a pricing relationship for the volatility parameter, using that premium and other inputs. A data vendor may deliver an implied-volatility field, and that field may be stored as a record in a database. The economic quantity it represents remains derived and model-dependent. Every assumption in the model rides along inside the number.

This is a specific instance of a general problem worth naming, because once you can see it you will see it constantly.

Proxy substitution happens when an analyst replaces a difficult question with an easier measurable one and then presents the easier answer as though it resolved the original. Volume stands in for liquidity. Open interest stands in for positioning. A volatility index stands in for fear. A moving average stands in for trend quality. An index return stands in for the condition of an entire market. In each case the substitution is invisible in the finished sentence, which is what makes it effective and what makes it dangerous.

Some things genuinely cannot be observed directly. Risk appetite, stress, crowding, fragility, and confidence are inferred from related evidence — spreads, depth, leverage, correlation, option prices, price impact, adjustment behavior. Inference is legitimate. What is not legitimate is presenting the inference with the status of an observation. Several complementary proxies may improve understanding; their agreement does not convert an inference into a fact.

Evidence needs a question

A measurement has no fixed evidentiary meaning on its own. It becomes evidence only when it is evaluated against a question, comparison, or hypothesis.

A widening spread may be strong evidence about a liquidity question. The same spread says very little about long-horizon valuation. Rising implied volatility is relevant to questions about option pricing, hedging demand, or event sensitivity, and it does not by itself prove fear, forecast realized volatility, or establish a mechanism.

A four-basis-point spread may indicate impaired conditions in one instrument and ordinary conditions in another. Its meaning depends on the market, the venue, the time of day, the size being traded, the prevailing variability, the historical range, and whether the quoted size is actually executable. The number does not explain itself.

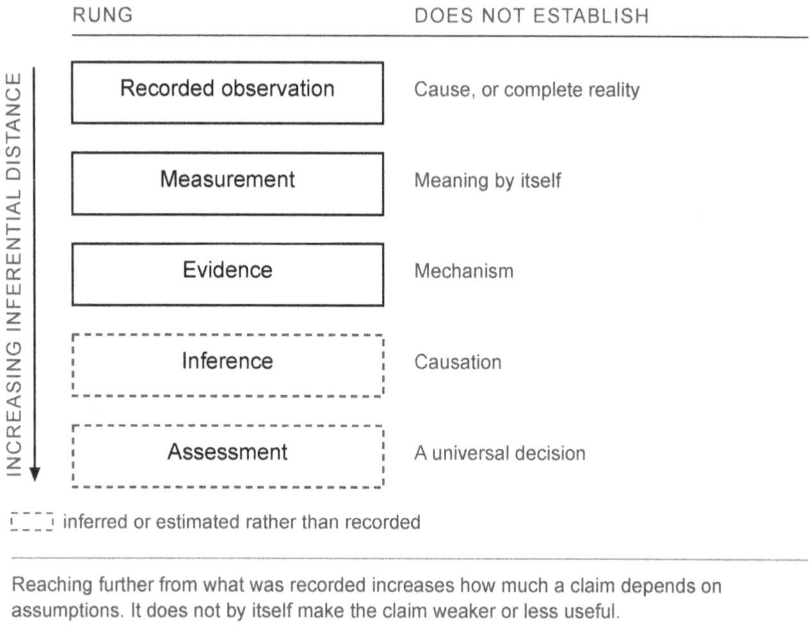

Figure 3. How far a claim reaches beyond what was recorded – and what each rung does not establish.

So the discipline is: before evaluating a measurement, state the question. Then state the baseline, the horizon, and the universe the claim is meant to cover. Most confident market statements fail at this step, and they fail quietly, because a missing baseline leaves no visible trace in the sentence.

Four things that are not the same as uncertainty

"Nothing is certain" is true, useless, and frequently a way of avoiding work. Several distinct conditions get flattened into it, and they demand different responses.

Condition	What it means	What to do about it
Uncertainty	The claim is not known with complete confidence	Qualify the confidence
Missing information	Potentially relevant evidence is unavailable	Do not silently treat absence as neutral
Measurement uncertainty	The representation is imperfect or method-sensitive	Report the method and its sensitivity
Model uncertainty	Alternative models or assumptions remain plausible	Compare specifications, or narrow the claim
Future uncertainty	The events have not happened yet	Use scenarios, not certainty
Error	A value, calculation, or assertion is wrong	Correct it, rather than lowering confidence

The last row matters most. Uncertainty can be legitimate; error demands correction. Downgrading a known mistake to "well, there's uncertainty" is not humility, it is concealment.

Two related rules follow. Missing data should not automatically become zero, unchanged, normal, or neutral — a missing component is not a balanced one. And a stale value is not a current one. Reusing a last-known number without saying so produces an assessment that looks complete and is materially misleading.

Two further failures are worth knowing by name because they appear in almost every impressive historical result you will ever be shown.

Survivorship bias arises when a dataset contains only what still exists today. Studying an index using today's members, applied backward, quietly removes the bankruptcies, the delistings, and the failures. It can substantially overstate returns, liquidity, and persistence.

Look-ahead bias arises when a study uses information that would not have been available at the moment the decision was supposedly made. Revised economic data, finalized index membership, complete option chains that did not exist in real time, and state labels assigned retrospectively all produce impressive and impossible results. Sorting records by date does not prevent it.

SIDEBAR

Confidence Is Not Certainty

Confidence attaches to a specific claim, not to an analysis as a whole. This sounds pedantic until you try it, and then it changes how you write.

Within one afternoon's work, an analyst can reasonably hold: high confidence that a price series is accurate; high confidence that realized variability increased; moderate confidence that the capacity to trade deteriorated; low confidence about the mechanism that produced it; and very low confidence about tomorrow's direction. Those are five different confidences, and collapsing them into "I'm fairly confident" destroys the information.

The dimensions worth keeping apart are confidence in the **data**, in the **measurement**, in the **description** of current conditions, in the proposed **mechanism**, in the **classification** being applied, and in any **prediction**. Descriptive confidence is often high while predictive confidence is very low, and that combination is normal rather than embarrassing.

Note also that confidence is not probability. A model may output a 60% probability while confidence in the model itself is low. And a number is not automatically more rigorous than a judgment: a meaningful probability requires a defined event, horizon, reference class, model, data, and calibration. A figure without those is decoration.

What actually determines how much confidence a conclusion deserves is not the quantity of supporting observations. It is their validity, relevance, independence, completeness, how far the claim reaches beyond what was measured, whether anything contradicts it, how much it depends on a model, and how well it distinguishes the favored explanation from the alternatives.

More indicators is not more evidence

That last point deserves separating out, because it is the most common way confidence gets manufactured.

A twenty-day moving average, a twenty-day rate of change, a trend regression, and a momentum oscillator may all appear on a chart as four independent confirmations. They are four transformations of one price series over one window. They will agree, and their agreement carries almost no additional information.

Evidence can be dependent through shared source data, shared transformation windows, shared model assumptions, common vendors, common market mechanisms, or duplicated exposures. **Indicator count is not evidence diversity.** Confidence should reflect independent information, not the number of panels displayed.

The useful version of this is triangulation: examining a question through measurements that are genuinely different in kind. Price, breadth, trading conditions, and cross-asset behavior tell you more jointly than four price derivatives ever will. The objective is not to maximize the number of indicators. It is to improve the diversity, independence, and relevance of the evidence.

Keeping more than one explanation alive

Responsible inquiry preserves more than one plausible account while the evidence permits it. Three roles are worth distinguishing.

A **primary hypothesis** organizes the current explanation. **Alternative hypotheses** capture competing mechanisms. A **null or minimal explanation** asks whether the pattern can be accounted for by ordinary variation, a measurement artifact, or a simpler process. The null explanation is the one that gets dropped, and it is often the correct answer.

Consider a case: an index rises while implied volatility also rises. This combination is mildly surprising, which makes it a magnet for confident stories. Several explanations are available.

- Concentrated demand for upside options, and the associated hedging, is amplifying the advance.
- Investors are participating in the advance while retaining downside protection.
- A scheduled event is raising option prices independently of any directional conviction.
- Reduced option supply is increasing the compensation required to bear volatility exposure.

- Nothing structural is happening; this is ordinary short-horizon variation.

The objective is not to invent every imaginable story. It is to compare explanations that would imply meaningfully different observations, and then to look for those observations. Evidence that is expected under one explanation and not under another is **discriminating**, and it is worth far more than evidence consistent with all of them.

Its counterpart is **negative evidence**: an observation expected under a hypothesis that fails to appear. Negative evidence is strong only when the observation process could actually have detected the thing. Failing to see participant-level activity in a dataset that does not contain participant-level activity is absence of evidence, not evidence of absence.

Finally, a hypothesis worth holding should identify what would weaken it. A claim that explains every outcome cannot be tested, and a claim that cannot be tested is a belief.

The distance from "it moved together" to "it caused it"

Causal language arrives early in market commentary and is almost never earned. The rungs between description and causation are worth naming.

Rung	The question	An example
Description	What occurred?	Price declined while realized variability rose.
Association	What moved together?	Declines were accompanied by variability expansion in this sample.
Sequence	What preceded what?	The option repricing preceded the largest interval of futures selling.
Mechanism	Through what process could influence occur?	Changing hedge sensitivity could produce additional futures transactions.
Contribution	Did the factor materially influence the outcome?	Hedging flow appears to have amplified the move.
Causation	Would the outcome have differed materially without it?	The factor caused a measurable portion of the decline.

Each rung requires more than the one below it. A coherent mechanism explains how an effect *could* occur; it does not establish that it did occur or that it dominated. Temporal order is necessary for causation and is rarely sufficient, particularly in markets where prices, variability, trading conditions, and hedging activity change nearly simultaneously, where different feeds use different clocks, and where some participants act before public information arrives.

It is also worth resisting the opposite failure. Market outcomes are frequently multicausal, but a longer list of possible causes is not a stronger explanation. Each factor assigned material weight needs evidence for that weight. It is better to say a factor was primary, contributing, amplifying, or incidental than to list six candidates and let the reader assume they all mattered.

Why a good story is not evidence

Narratives organize observations into sequences, and human beings find sequences convincing. That is exactly the problem.

A central-bank announcement followed by a decline is a real temporal relationship and a weak causal one. Positioning, trading conditions, other simultaneous events, prior expectations, and what happened over the following week may all change the explanation. Proximity in time is not a mechanism.

A responsible narrative labels each of its links: observed, measured, estimated, inferred, assumed, or unresolved. Most published market narratives contain at least one link that is assumed and presented as observed, and identifying which one is a genuinely useful reading skill.

Narrative coherence is not evidentiary support. A narrative is a structured hypothesis whose links must be traceable and revisable, and the more satisfying it is, the harder it will be to revise.

SIDEBAR

Narrative Coherence Is Not Evidence

Take a market explanation apart link by link and label each one. There are six labels, and only the first two are things anyone saw.

Observed — a source reported it. **Measured** — it was calculated from records by a defined method. **Estimated** — a model produced it. **Inferred** — it was reasoned to from other things. **Assumed** — it was taken as given, without evidence in this account. **Unresolved** — the account does not say, and may not know.

Now run the labels across a sentence of the kind published every day:

> *Dealers were short gamma, so as the market fell they had to sell, which accelerated the decline into thin afternoon liquidity.*

"Dealers were short gamma" is **estimated** — it depends on assumptions about who owned which side, what was netted internally, and what was offset elsewhere. "They had to sell" is **assumed**; a sensitivity is not an obligation. "Which accelerated the decline" is **inferred**, and it is the causal claim doing all the work. "Thin afternoon liquidity" is **measured**, if anyone measured it, and **assumed** if nobody did.

One sentence. One measurement, at best. Everything else is estimate, assumption, and inference presented in the grammar of observation — and the grammar is what makes it persuasive, because English does not mark the difference.

This is not an argument against narratives. Organizing observations into a sequence is how anyone understands anything. It is an argument for labeling the links, and for noticing that **the most satisfying account is usually the one with the most unlabeled assumptions in it** — satisfaction comes from the gaps being smoothed over, not from their being filled.

A useful habit: when an explanation feels complete, look for the link that would be hardest to check. That is almost always the one carrying the conclusion.

Language that matches the evidence

Because it is so easy to upgrade a claim by accident, it is worth having explicit vocabulary for each level of support.

When the evidence is	Say
Direct and well bounded	records, shows, establishes
Supported but not proven	indicates, supports, is consistent with
Limited or indirect	may reflect, could indicate, remains possible
Unresolved	cannot be determined, evidence is mixed, remains provisional

The rule holds in both directions. Data may confirm that a displayed spread widened. They generally cannot confirm that investors panicked. And words like manipulation, panic, conviction, capitulation, accumulation, and distribution require an operational definition and supporting evidence before they mean anything at all.

Note too that shortening a sentence can silently upgrade it. Compressing "may be consistent with increased sensitivity around those strike prices" into "shows increased sensitivity" saves six words and changes the claim. Where a qualification is doing work, it stays.

What this looks like in practice

Consider a specific case. At eleven in the morning, a capitalization-weighted equity index is up 1.1%. Implied volatility is also higher. Only 42% of the index's components are advancing. A handful of large technology companies account for most of the gain. Futures volume is elevated, visible spreads look normal, and activity in call options expiring this week is unusually high.

The question. Does this represent a broad market expansion, or a concentrated directional event?

What is recorded and measured. The capitalization-weighted index is higher. Equal-weight and sector participation are weak. Leadership is concentrated. Short-dated implied volatility and call activity are elevated. Futures volume is elevated. Visible spreads are normal, but depth, price impact, and recovery evidence are incomplete.

Competing explanations. Broad repricing toward risk. Large-cap leadership without broad participation. Short-horizon amplification connected to options activity. Event-sensitive positioning ahead of a scheduled announcement. Or ordinary short-horizon variation.

Additional evidence. The equal-weighted index is nearly flat. Most sectors are unchanged or lower. Call activity is concentrated in same-week expirations. Model-dependent estimates of dealer exposure suggest sensitivity near current prices. Liquidity appears functional for the sizes actually being traded. A major earnings announcement is scheduled after the close.

The assessment. The capitalization-weighted index is advancing, but the move is narrowly concentrated and is not presently confirmed by equal-weight or broad sector participation. Short-dated option activity and the model-dependent exposure estimates are consistent with possible options-related amplification, although who initiated the trades, who owns which side, and what the net exposure is all remain uncertain. Visible spreads are normal, but the broader liquidity evidence is incomplete. The best description is a concentrated, event-sensitive advance rather than a broadly supported expansion. Confidence in that description is moderate; confidence in the mechanism and in any prediction is lower.

What would change it. The broad-expansion reading would strengthen if participation, equal-weight performance, and sector leadership broaden and persist after the event. The temporary-amplification reading would strengthen if call activity fades, leadership stays narrow, the exposure estimates decline, and the index reverses after the announcement. Confidence would fall if the option data become stale, if the ownership assumptions prove unstable, or if the liquidity evidence conflicts materially.

Notice what that assessment does not do. It does not say the market is bullish. It does not predict the close. It does not tell anybody to do anything. It states what is supported, at what confidence, and what would change it — which is both less than the confident version and considerably more useful, because you can check it tomorrow.

Knowledge that stays open

Everything in this chapter points toward one commitment. It has a name in the scholarly framework — the principle of provisional knowledge — and it is worth stating plainly, because it is frequently misunderstood.

Market understanding is the current best-supported account permitted by available evidence, measurements, models, assumptions, and scope. It remains open to revision when stronger evidence, improved measurements, better explanations, or changed conditions justify it.

This is not a licence for vagueness. Evidence can justify strong conclusions. Some explanations are better supported than others. Some measurements are more valid, some models are better calibrated, and some claims are simply wrong. Humility means recognizing the scope and conditions of a conclusion, preserving plausible alternatives while the evidence is incomplete, and being willing to revise. It does not mean treating every interpretation as equally valid or declining to conclude anything.

The corollary is that correction is not embarrassing. Changing an assessment because the evidence changed is the process working. A framework that cannot admit error stops being a way of investigating markets and becomes a doctrine about them.

Takeaway

The sentence at the top of this chapter had a fact in it, and everything else was a claim of a different kind wearing the fact's clothing. Almost all market commentary works this way, and most of it is not dishonest — it is just compressed past the point where the difference is visible.

The ladder from record to measurement to evidence to inference to assessment is not academic apparatus. It is the only reliable way to find out which parts of a confident statement you actually have reason to believe. Measurements are constructed, not found. Evidence requires a question. Confidence belongs to specific claims. Alternatives stay alive until something rules them out. And a compelling story is a hypothesis, not a finding.

With that in place, we can look at what is worth measuring. The next chapter introduces four different ways of looking at the same market, and the first thing it does is explain what they are not.

PART TWO

Market Understanding

Chapters 3–8

> The question is not what the market is doing. It is under what conditions it is doing it.

The middle of this book proposes four ways of looking at any market: what it can absorb, what participants are still carrying, how much prices are moving, and whether direction has persisted.

Four chapters take these one at a time, because each has its own vocabulary, its own measurements, and its own characteristic ways of being misread. Liquidity is confused with volume. Positioning is confused with sentiment. Volatility is confused with fear. Trend is confused with a force acting on prices.

The separation is deliberate and temporary. Markets do not experience capacity, exposure, variability, and direction independently, and the most important information is usually in how the four are arranged relative to one another rather than in any of them alone.

Chapter 8 puts them back together. It is where the argument of Part I finally does concrete work, and it introduces the term the rest of the book depends on.

CHAPTER THREE

Four Ways to Look at a Market

The screen problem

Ask someone who follows markets closely what they look at, and you will usually get a list. Price, volume, a couple of moving averages, a volatility index, some options data, breadth, maybe a positioning report on Fridays. The list grows over time, because every time something surprising happens, the natural response is to add whatever would have shown it.

The result is a screen that contains a great deal of information and very little structure. Any position can be defended by selecting a favorable subset. Nothing in the arrangement says which observations belong together, which are measuring the same thing twice, or what any of them can establish on its own.

The opposite failure is equally common and shorter: pick one favored indicator and let it stand for the market. That produces confidence at the cost of being wrong in a specific and repeatable way.

What is missing in both cases is a way of organizing observations by *what dimension of the market they illuminate.* That is what this part of the book provides. It proposes four categories, and it is careful about what they are.

What a category like this actually is

An **observational domain** is a conceptual category used to organize evidence about one dimension of market behavior. It gives related observations a shared home and a stable vocabulary, while keeping the distinction between what exists in the market and how it is being measured.

The plain-English word for this is **perspective** — a way of looking at a market. That is what the four are, and the rest of this book will often call them that. *Observational domain* is the term the framework uses, and it is worth knowing, because it is doing something the everyday word does not: it names the category as belonging to the observer rather than to the market.

That definition is doing more work by exclusion than by inclusion. Five boundaries follow from it, and every one of them is a place where market commentary routinely goes wrong.

A domain is not the phenomenon. Liquidity is a property of a market's capacity to accommodate exchange. The liquidity domain is the analytical category in which evidence about that capacity is organized. The map is not the territory, and the filing cabinet is not the map.

A domain is not a measurement. A bid–ask spread, quoted depth, an estimate of price impact, and the time an order book takes to rebuild may all provide evidence about liquidity. None of them is liquidity. Each represents selected characteristics of something broader.

A domain is not an indicator or index. An indicator combines or transforms measurements according to a rule. A domain remains a category even when no number has been assigned to it — which is often the honest situation.

A domain is not a causal force. This one matters enough to be blunt about. Conditions in one domain may influence another, but the category does not act on the market. It is tempting to write about "the four forces driving markets," because that is a sentence with momentum in it. It is also a claim about causation that the evidence does not support, and it converts a way of looking into a set of hidden actors. The word *force* can be useful when describing pressure, influence, or feedback within a market. It should not replace the more careful word *domain*.

A domain is not a predictive model. Sorting evidence into four categories does not determine what a price will do next. Prediction requires additional assumptions, definitions, estimation, validation, and explicit handling of uncertainty. None of that comes free with a filing system.

Hold those five in mind through the next four chapters, and this part of the book will be useful. Lose them, and you will have acquired a more sophisticated vocabulary for making the same mistakes.

It may help to see where a domain sits relative to everything around it. Using liquidity as the running example:

Concept	What it is	Liquidity example
Phenomenon	The aspect of market reality being studied	A market's ability to absorb transactions
Data	Recorded events or reported values	Bid, ask, size, trade price, timestamp
Measurement	A defined representation built from data	The bid–ask spread; an estimate of price impact
Evidence	A measurement interpreted as relevant to a claim	Persistently widening spreads support concern about weakening capacity
Observational domain	The category organizing related evidence	Liquidity
Interpretation	A reasoned statement about what the evidence may mean	Exchange capacity is deteriorating at the current horizon
Model	A selective representation used to describe, estimate, or classify	A liquidity classifier built from spread, depth, and recovery

Seven rows, and only one of them is the thing itself. The domain sits in the middle: above the measurements, below the interpretation, and not identical to either.

Why these four

The four are **liquidity**, **positioning**, **volatility**, and **trend**. They were not derived from a discovery that market reality divides naturally into four parts. They are a design choice: an attempt to find a small set of categories broad enough to organize most of what matters and distinct enough to keep their meanings separate.

Each addresses a different foundational question.

Domain	The question it asks	What it attends to
Liquidity	What is this market's current capacity to accommodate exchange?	Immediacy, cost, depth, price impact, resilience
Positioning	How is exposure distributed, and where are sensitivities concentrated?	Holdings, leverage, inventory, hedging needs, option sensitivities
Volatility	How is uncertainty being expressed through prices and option valuations?	Realized movement, implied expectations, asymmetry, term structure
Trend	What directional persistence is emerging through time?	Direction, persistence, breadth, participation, leadership

Put more plainly: **capacity, exposure, variability, direction.**

The four questions are complementary rather than overlapping. Liquidity concerns what the market *can absorb*. Positioning concerns what participants are *still carrying*. Volatility concerns *how much prices are moving and in what pattern*. Trend concerns *whether that movement has been going somewhere*. Together they provide a vocabulary for describing a market without reducing it to price.

There is also a practical reason for stopping at four. Too few categories collapse genuinely different phenomena into one label. Too many become impossible to apply consistently, produce overlapping classifications, and obscure more than they organize.

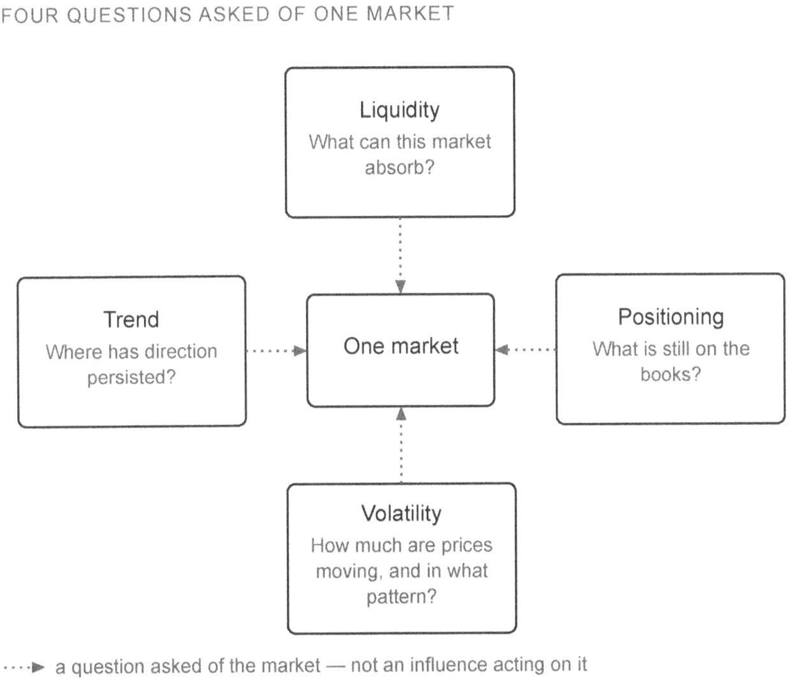

Four ways of looking, drawn at the same size and the same distance because none ranks above another. They are the foundational four, not the only four, and they are not forces acting on prices.

Figure 4. Four questions asked of one market. Ways of looking, not forces acting on prices.

What the four are not: the honest version

Parsimony is not the same as completeness, and this is the point at which a retail treatment of a framework usually starts overselling. So, plainly:

These four do not exhaust market reality. Funding and collateral conditions, credit transmission, information flow, participation structure, and institutional design may in some contexts deserve separate treatment. Whether they are best handled as additional domains, as sub-parts of existing ones, as influences that cut across all four, or as external conditions is an open question that research has not settled.

They are described as *foundational* rather than *complete*: a starting architecture, proposed because it is useful, and revisable when evidence says it should be. The conclusion of this book returns to what would justify changing it.

It is worth being equally clear about what the framework does not do on its own. By itself, organizing evidence into these four categories does not:

- calculate a market state;
- assign weights to measurements;
- determine whether a domain's condition is favorable or unfavorable;
- generate entry or exit indications;
- predict direction, return, or variability;
- establish causation merely by categorizing evidence;
- guarantee completeness, or eliminate uncertainty.

A model might later use evidence from these four domains to estimate how a market is arranged, classify it, monitor change, or support a decision. That model would be a separate thing, requiring its own inputs, transformations, assumptions, thresholds, validation, and documented failure modes. A model does not become valid because its inputs have been sorted into well-named boxes.

This boundary protects the framework from being judged by claims it does not make. It also stops models from borrowing authority they have not earned.

SIDEBAR

What a Model Is, and Isn't

The word *model* covers everything from a sentence about how two things relate to a system with a hundred million parameters. What they share is more useful than what separates them.

A model is a simplified, purpose-specific representation of selected features of a system. Every model selects some information, imposes structure, and omits the rest. That is not a defect. It is the mechanism by which a model becomes useful at all: it can help precisely because it leaves out complexity irrelevant to its purpose.

Five things follow, and they are the questions worth asking of any model anyone shows you.

What is it for? A model cannot be judged without knowing what it was designed to do. A model that describes current conditions accurately may have no predictive value whatsoever, and that is not a failure unless someone claimed otherwise. Purpose comes before evaluation.

What did it leave out? Omission is unavoidable. Hidden omission is not. Every model is a statement about what its designer believed mattered.

Is the output an observation or an inference? An inferred quantity should never be presented with the standing of a directly observed fact. Fragility, crowding, stress, dealer exposure, and market state are all inferred. When one of them arrives as a number on a screen, the number is a model output.

Does correct arithmetic mean a correct model? No. A model can be implemented perfectly and still be conceptually wrong, and mathematical form can make assumptions more visible without making them true. Confirming that the code does what the specification says is a different activity from asking whether the specification made sense.

Do several models agreeing mean more than one? Only if they are actually independent. Several models built on the same data, the same features, and the same assumptions do not constitute confirmation. They constitute one model, reported four times.

One more, which applies to everything in this book: a stable calculation does not guarantee a stable meaning. A model whose code has not changed in five years may nonetheless have quietly stopped measuring what it used to measure, because the market it points at has changed.

The boundaries between the four are not sealed

A single measurement can provide evidence about more than one domain, and the significance of one domain often depends on the condition of the others.

A **bid–ask spread** is primarily liquidity evidence, and it may widen because variability rose or because market makers reduced risk in response to their inventory. **Open interest** is primarily positioning evidence, and it may shape future demand for liquidity and future sensitivity to price movement. The **implied-volatility skew** — the difference in implied volatility between options at different strike prices — is primarily volatility evidence, and it may also reflect protective positioning, dealer inventory, or demand around a scheduled event. **Market breadth** is primarily trend evidence, and it may reveal concentration that has consequences for liquidity.

Permeability does not make the categories meaningless. It reflects how markets actually work. The point of classification is not to pretend an observation has only one possible reading. It is to make explicit which dimension you are examining, disclose what else the observation might mean, and avoid counting the same information twice when observations are later combined.

The right posture is disciplined flexibility. A rigid classification rule creates false precision; no structure at all creates inconsistency.

Distinct, but not independent

Markets do not experience these four separately, and the interactions carry information that no individual domain contains.

Concentrated exposure may sit quietly for months while trading capacity is deep, and become consequential the moment that capacity thins. Rising variability may be absorbed without much directional effect when exposure is balanced and the market can accommodate the resulting trades. A persistent trend may attract additional exposure, increasing concentration and future sensitivity — so that the trend's own success changes the conditions it operates in.

This is why isolated indicators mislead. A low volatility reading does not establish stability. A strong trend does not establish healthy participation. A large position does not imply imminent pressure. A high-volume market is not necessarily liquid for the size you actually want to trade.

The meaning of any one domain depends partly on the condition of the others. Understanding a market therefore requires reading across them rather than reading indicators in isolation. Chapter 8 is devoted to exactly that, and the four chapters between here and there are the necessary preparation.

Where this framework can fail

A framework should be examined most carefully where it appears most foundational, because everything downstream inherits its errors. The following are part of the framework rather than objections to it.

Important market phenomena may not fit clearly into any of the four. Domain boundaries can become ambiguous when one measurement reflects several mechanisms at once. The structure can encourage counting the same evidence twice. A domain with abundant data may get more attention than a domain that matters more but is harder to observe — a bias toward what is available rather than what is important. The same measurement can mean different things across instruments, venues, and horizons. And a well-chosen label can create the appearance of understanding while the measurements beneath it remain weak or heavily model-dependent.

There is one more thing worth saying, because a retail treatment of any framework tends to leave it out. **This architecture has not been validated.** It is a scholarly proposition. Whether four domains organize evidence better than some other arrangement, whether they are genuinely distinct rather than redundant, whether multidomain assessment improves description or decisions compared with simpler methods — these are research questions with open status, not settled findings. The framework earns its place if the added structure improves understanding enough to justify itself, and that case has not been closed.

None of the four concepts is an invention of this framework, either. Liquidity, positioning, volatility, and trend are deeply established in financial economics, market microstructure, derivatives research, portfolio management, and quantitative analysis, with extensive literatures behind each. What is being proposed here is their organization as complementary observational domains within one architecture for reasoning. That is a contribution of arrangement, not of discovery, and saying so is not modesty. It is accuracy.

Takeaway

Four questions, asked of the same market at the same time: What can it absorb? What is still on the books? How much are prices moving, and in what pattern? Where has direction persisted?

They are perspectives, not forces. Ways of looking, not things acting. They organize evidence rather than generating conclusions. They are foundational rather than complete, and the architecture is open to revision if the evidence warrants it.

Their boundaries are useful but permeable, and the meaning of each depends on the condition of the others. **No one perspective is enough** — which is why the four chapters that follow are, in an important sense, incomplete until Chapter 8 puts them back together.

We begin with the one that determines whether any intention can become a transaction at all.

CHAPTER FOUR

Liquidity: Can the Market Actually Trade?

The gap between deciding and doing

Every market opinion has a hidden assumption attached to it: that the position implied by the opinion can actually be established, adjusted, or exited on terms close to the ones on the screen.

Most of the time that assumption holds so reliably that nobody notices it. A retail-sized order fills instantly at the quoted price. The screen looks like the market, and the market looks available.

The assumption becomes visible in two situations. The first is size: the same instrument that absorbed ten thousand shares without a flicker behaves entirely differently when asked to absorb five hundred thousand. The second is stress: the moment when a large number of participants want to do the same thing at the same time, and discover collectively that the capacity they were counting on was partly the same capacity.

Liquidity is the name for that capacity. It is the first of the four domains, and it goes first because nothing else in a market matters if intentions cannot become transactions.

The usual definition, and what it leaves out

Liquidity is commonly described as the ability to buy or sell an asset without materially affecting its price. That is a reasonable place to start and it is incomplete, because it does not say *how much* you are trying to trade, *how quickly*, *where*, *which side*, or *under what conditions*.

A fuller statement:

> **Liquidity is a market's capacity to accommodate exchange with a given degree of immediacy, cost, depth, price impact, and resilience, under specified conditions.**

The shorter version — liquidity is a market's capacity for exchange — carries the central idea. The longer version carries the conditions under which the capacity has to be evaluated, and the conditions are where all the difficulty lives.

Two consequences follow immediately.

Liquidity is a capacity, not an event. A completed transaction demonstrates that exchange occurred. It does not reveal how much more could have occurred, at what cost, how quickly, or with what effect on price. Liquidity concerns readiness, not history.

Liquidity exists in degrees, and in directions. A market can be highly liquid for one order size and poorly liquid for another. It can function well in ordinary conditions and be impaired in stress. It can offer strong buying capacity and weak selling capacity at the same moment. It can work adequately for a participant who can wait several hours and fail entirely for one who cannot.

Seven things a liquidity claim has to specify

Because liquidity is conditional rather than a fixed property of an instrument, a claim about it is incomplete until it names its conditions. There are seven, and skipping any of them produces a statement that sounds informative and is not.

1. **Instrument.** What is actually being exchanged. A company's stock, a specific futures contract month, one option strike.
2. **Venue.** Where the exchange can occur, and whether capacity is split across several places.
3. **Size.** How large the intended trade is relative to available capacity. This is the condition most often omitted and the one that changes the answer most.
4. **Side.** Buying, selling, borrowing, lending, or hedging. These are not symmetric.
5. **Urgency.** Whether execution must happen now or can be worked through time.
6. **Horizon.** Seconds, minutes, a session, or longer.
7. **Market condition.** Ordinary, event-driven, stressed, or structurally impaired.

A stock may be liquid for a retail order and illiquid for a block. A futures contract may be liquid in its nearest expiration and thin in distant months. An option may be liquid at one strike and not another. A government bond may trade efficiently under normal conditions and become difficult during a funding shock.

This is why "is it liquid?" is not a well-formed question, and why anybody who answers it without asking what you are trying to do has not understood it.

The dimensions that can move independently

Liquidity has parts, and the parts do not move together. This is precisely why no single number represents it.

Dimension	The question it answers
Immediacy	How quickly can the exchange occur?
Cost	What explicit and implicit cost comes with it?
Depth	How much quantity is available near current prices?
Price impact	How much does executing move the market?
Resilience	How quickly do price and available quantity recover afterward?

A market can have narrow spreads and very little depth. It can offer substantial depth and recover slowly after a large trade. It can fill orders instantly while imposing large price impact. Three further characteristics matter and are usually folded into resilience in practice: how consistently prices and counterparties remain available through time, how quickly new interest appears after existing interest is consumed, and how the available quantity is distributed across price levels rather than concentrated at the best one.

A single "liquidity score" that combines these will move for reasons you cannot see, which is a general problem with composites and one we return to in Chapter 9.

Liquidity is not volume

This is the most common confusion in the domain, and it runs in both directions.

Trading volume records transactions that already happened. Liquidity concerns capacity for transactions that have not happened yet. Related, not synonymous.

A market may show very high volume precisely because many participants are transacting under stress, while spreads widen, depth disappears, and price impact grows. In that case the high volume is a *consequence* of deteriorating capacity, not evidence of abundant capacity.

Conversely, a market may show modest volume while maintaining narrow effective costs, adequate depth for the sizes actually being traded, low price impact, and rapid replenishment. For your purposes that market may be considerably more liquid than the busy one.

	Market A	Market B
Daily activity	High volume	Lower volume
Spread	Wide	Narrow
Depth near current price	Shallow	Adequate for typical size
Price impact	Large	Small
Recovery after trades	Slow	Rapid
Reasonable reading	High activity, weak capacity	Lower activity, stronger capacity

Volume becomes useful evidence when it is interpreted alongside cost, depth, impact, and recovery. On its own it is a measure of how much has happened, which is a different question from how much can happen.

Where liquidity comes from, and why it leaves

Liquidity is not supplied by one kind of participant. It emerges from the combined behavior of natural buyers and sellers, market makers, dealers, arbitrageurs, hedgers, institutions, execution algorithms, and anyone managing inventory or funding needs.

The participants who supply it are accepting risks in exchange for compensation. They may hold inventory while prices move against them. They may transact against someone who knows more than they do. They may need financing for positions they are carrying. Their willingness to keep supplying capacity declines when uncertainty rises, when their inventory becomes unbalanced, when funding tightens, when related markets become unstable, when risk limits bind, or when expected variability increases.

Read that list again with one question in mind: when do those conditions occur together? The answer is the important one. **Capacity can decline precisely when the largest number of participants need it.** This is not a conspiracy or a failure of anyone's obligations. It follows from the fact that the people supplying capacity face the same conditions as the people demanding it.

Demand for liquidity is adaptive too. Participants accelerate execution when prices move against them, reduce urgency when costs rise, split orders across time and venues, or substitute related instruments. Both sides respond to conditions, which means liquidity is not a fixed inventory that can be counted once and assumed to remain.

What you can see, and what you get

The liquidity visible before you trade is not necessarily the liquidity you experience while trading. Five forms are worth keeping distinct.

Displayed liquidity is visible interest represented in quotes and orders. It may be cancelled, moved, fragmented, or simply gone by the time an order reaches it.

Hidden liquidity is interest not fully visible in advance. It cannot be inferred reliably from what is displayed.

Realized liquidity is the execution conditions actually experienced. It is known only during or after execution, and it depends on how the order was worked.

Latent liquidity is potential willingness to transact that may appear if price or conditions change. Difficult to measure and usually model-dependent.

Committed liquidity is capacity contractually or institutionally expected from dealers or facilities. Commitments have limits and conditions, and can fail under extreme stress.

The practical consequence: displayed depth should not be treated as guaranteed executable capacity, and a thin displayed book does not prove that no further capacity exists. Both errors are common, and they push in opposite directions.

From a number to a conclusion

Here is what the ladder from Chapter 2 looks like when applied to a specific liquidity observation.

Rung	The liquidity case
Record	Recorded bid and ask quotations
Measurement	The quoted spread
Observation	The spread widened from 2 basis points to 8 — a basis point being one hundredth of one percent
Evidence claim	Observable trading cost appears to be increasing
Interpretation	Capacity may be deteriorating for the size, venue, and horizon being evaluated
Qualification	The change may be temporary, venue-specific, event-driven, or based on stale quotes, and may be offset by hidden depth and rapid replenishment

The interpretation gets stronger when the widening spread coincides with reduced depth, greater price impact, slower replenishment, and impaired recovery. It gets weaker when the change is brief, isolated to one venue, or contradicted by other evidence.

A fuller version of the same exercise: an analyst wanting to know whether liquidity in an equity-index futures market is deteriorating might find that the spread widened from one tick to two, that depth near the best prices fell 40%, that comparable orders moved price further than before, that the order book took longer to rebuild, and that displayed orders were being cancelled more quickly as price approached them.

The disciplined conclusion is not "liquidity is bad." It is: *liquidity appears to have deteriorated relative to the normal range for this time of day, because spreads widened, near-touch depth declined, comparable price impact increased, and recovery slowed. Hidden liquidity and future participant response remain uncertain.*

That sentence is longer, and it can be checked.

Three stages of the same market

The clearest way to see conditionality is to hold the instrument constant and change only the demand placed on it.

Stage one: an ordinary transaction. A participant wants to sell ten thousand shares. The spread is narrow, depth is sufficient, execution happens quickly, the average price stays close to where the market was, and depth replenishes afterward. The supported claim is narrow and correct: liquidity is functional for that size, that venue, and that horizon, under current conditions.

Stage two: a larger transaction. The same participant wants to sell five hundred thousand shares. Available depth is insufficient. The order has to be divided. The average execution price is worse. Price moves materially as the size is completed. Nothing about the company changed. Nothing about the market structure changed. The *relationship* between the intended exchange and the available capacity changed, and that relationship is what liquidity is.

Stage three: concentrated demand. Several participants attempt to sell at once. Variability rises. Those supplying capacity reduce their quoted size. Spreads widen. Depth disappears. Price impact stops being proportional to size and starts accelerating. Recovery slows. The demand for exchange has become concentrated at exactly the moment the capacity to absorb it is declining.

Notice what would have failed to capture stage three: historical average volume, and a spread that was narrow yesterday. Both are backward-looking measurements of a capacity that is conditional on circumstances that have now changed.

SAME ASSET

ORDINARY SIZE	LARGE SIZE	STRESS DEMAND
10,000 shares	500,000 shares	several participants sell at once
— spread narrow, depth sufficient	— available depth insufficient	— liquidity suppliers reduce quoted size
— execution occurs quickly	— the order must be divided	— price impact becomes nonlinear
— depth replenishes after the trade	— price moves materially as size is completed	— recovery slows

The asset has not changed; the liquidity relationship has. The three panels are conditions, not a sequence, and none of the quantities here is a threshold at which liquidity breaks.

Figure 5. The same asset under three different transaction demands. The asset has not changed; the liquidity relationship has.

What stress reveals

Liquidity often looks abundant right up until many participants try to use it simultaneously. Stress is informative because it reveals whether apparently independent sources of capacity were actually independent, or whether they depend on participants who withdraw under the same conditions.

Stress may expose correlation among liquidity demands that looked unrelated; the withdrawal of dealer and market-making capacity; execution delays and lower fill probability; large gaps between displayed and executable prices; forced selling, hedging, or deleveraging; and discontinuous price adjustment with slow recovery.

Thinking about this in advance is worthwhile, and it has a firm limit. Examining how a market might behave under stress cannot reveal the future. What it can do is identify assumptions unlikely to hold when participation, variability, funding, and risk-bearing capacity all change together — which is the situation in which those assumptions matter.

Common misreadings

	The misreading
Volume means liquidity	Volume records completed activity, not future capacity
Narrow spreads prove liquidity	Spreads can be narrow while depth and continuity are weak
Liquidity is a property of the asset	It depends on size, urgency, venue, side, horizon, and conditions
Displayed depth is available depth	Displayed orders can cancel, move, or fragment
Stable prices prove liquidity	Prices may be stable because activity is low and capacity untested
Yesterday's liquidity is today's	Participation and risk-bearing capacity are adaptive

To which two more should be added, because they are subtler. Comparing liquidity across instruments without normalizing for price, contract size, venue, and convention produces meaningless comparisons. And treating a composite liquidity estimate as a direct observation hides the assumptions inside it, along with the possibility that its components are pointing in opposite directions.

What liquidity cannot tell you

Liquidity explains an important dimension of how a market functions. It does not determine value, direction, or outcome. On its own, liquidity analysis cannot establish whether prices are correct, whether a trend will continue, whether variability will rise or fall, what an information event meant, whether a reaction is temporary or permanent, or whether observed deterioration is the cause of a price move, a consequence of it, or both at once.

That last one is worth sitting with. In a market under pressure, capacity and prices move together, and the direction of influence is frequently indeterminate from the outside. An explanation that confidently assigns causation in either direction is claiming more than the evidence supports.

Liquidity measurements are also incomplete, often venue-specific, sometimes delayed, and frequently model-dependent or sensitive to how execution was measured. Those limitations should constrain the scope and confidence of any conclusion drawn from them.

Why it matters anyway

Liquidity determines whether intentions can become transactions. It influences transaction cost, capital allocation, risk transfer, execution quality, and how reliably prices reflect anything at all.

Well-informed participants may be unable to express a view when capacity is weak. Abundant capacity can allow very large changes in ownership and risk to occur with little visible disruption. So liquidity is more than an execution detail. It is a dimension of how a market functions and of how fragile it may be.

It is not, however, a measure of market health, and it is not an independent predictor of direction. A deeply liquid market can decline. An illiquid one can rise. The domain answers a specific question, and answering it well requires not asking it to answer others.

Takeaway

Liquidity is a market's capacity to accommodate exchange, and it is conditional on what you are trying to do. Not a property of the asset, not synonymous with volume, not visible in full from a screen, and not stable through time.

It has parts that move independently, which is why one number cannot represent it. It is supplied by participants who face the same pressures as the people demanding it, which is why it can thin precisely when it is most needed. And what is displayed is not what will be experienced.

What liquidity establishes is whether the market can absorb what participants want to do. Whether they will want to do it, and how much they are still carrying, is the next chapter's question.

CHAPTER FIVE

Positioning: What Is Still on the Books

Prices tell you what already happened

A price is the record of a transaction that has been completed. It tells you the terms on which two participants were willing to exchange something at a particular moment.

What it does not tell you is what remains. After that transaction, somebody owns something they did not own before. Somebody is financing it. Somebody has an obligation that now behaves differently if prices move. Somebody may be a little closer to a limit that will compel them to act.

None of that is visible in the price, and all of it affects what happens next.

Positioning is the domain that attends to what is still on the books. It is the hardest of the four to observe and, for that reason, the one most prone to confident overstatement.

What positioning is

Positioning is the distribution of financial exposure, sensitivity, leverage, concentration, and potential adjustment requirements across market participants, under specified conditions.

The phrase *under specified conditions* is not decoration. A position's significance depends on the instrument, the participant, the time horizon, how it is financed, what liquidity is available, how variable prices are, what risk limits apply, and which variables the exposure is actually sensitive to.

A position is not important because it is large. It becomes analytically important when its structure makes the holder, or the market, sensitive to changing conditions.

Four related ideas are worth separating, because they get used interchangeably and are not the same.

Concept	What it means	Example
Position	A contractual, ownership, or inventory quantity held	One million shares; five thousand futures contracts
Economic exposure	The overall gain-and-loss relationship after related holdings, hedges, financing, and obligations	A long equity holding offset by short futures may carry far less directional exposure than the share count suggests
Sensitivity	How the value or management requirement changes as market variables change	How much an option portfolio's value moves per unit move in the underlying
Adjustment requirement	A condition under which the holder may need to hedge, rebalance, finance, reduce, or increase	A margin call; an allocation breach; an option expiration

A reported position can differ enormously from a participant's actual economic exposure. A futures position may hedge a cash holding. An option position may be one leg of a spread. A dealer may offset customer exposure in a different instrument on a different venue. A portfolio that looks strongly directional in one dataset may be close to neutral once the complete structure is visible — and the complete structure is almost never visible.

Three things positioning is not

Positioning is not price. Rising prices do not establish that participants are broadly long, and falling prices do not establish that they are bearish. A price increase may come from new buying, from traders closing losing short positions, from hedging, from forced buying, or simply from thin conditions. Two markets can trade at the same price with entirely different exposure structures. Positioning can also change substantially while price barely moves, when transactions transfer risk without producing a directional result.

Positioning is not flow. Flow is activity through time; positioning is what remains after the activity. A purchase may open a new long position, close a short one, hedge something else, rebalance an index, or facilitate a client. The same observed flow can produce entirely different changes in exposure. Open interest may rise when both sides establish new contracts, remain unchanged when exposure transfers from one participant to another, or fall when both sides close — and even then the directional meaning stays uncertain without knowing the complete structure.

Positioning is not sentiment or intent. A position does not reveal why it is held. Long exposure may reflect optimism. It may equally reflect index replication, matching a liability, arbitrage, facilitating a customer, managing inventory, a regulatory requirement, a tax consideration, or a hedge against something else entirely. Short exposure may reflect a negative view, or it may hedge a long cash position, offset option risk, support market making, or express a relative-value trade.

That third one is the source of most bad positioning commentary. Turning every reported long into a bull and every reported short into a bear is not analysis. It is translation into a language the data does not speak.

The dimensions that matter

	Dimension
Direction	Indicates the sign and structure of sensitivity — not the holder's motive
Gross versus net	Large gross exposure can create substantial sensitivity even when net exposure is small
Concentration	Exposure held by relatively few participants, instruments, or strikes can produce correlated adjustment
Crowding	Similar exposures, assumptions, or response rules across participants can produce synchronized behavior
Leverage	Higher leverage reduces tolerance for adverse movement and can force adjustment
Convexity	Exposure whose sensitivity itself changes as conditions change can generate accelerating hedging needs

Three further characteristics matter and are frequently overlooked: the horizon over which an exposure must be managed, which determines when expirations and mandates force action; dependence on continued financing, which can convert an otherwise stable position into urgent demand for liquidity; and how broadly exposure is dispersed across participants rather than held by a small group.

The gross-versus-net distinction deserves a number. Suppose one group of participants holds ten billion dollars of long exposure and another holds nine point eight billion of short exposure. Net exposure is two hundred million, which sounds negligible. Gross exposure is nineteen point eight billion, and both sides carry financing costs, risk limits, and potential adjustment pressure.

A nearly balanced net measure can coexist with enormous leverage, substantial option sensitivity, and considerable capacity for both sides to need to trade at once. Reporting only the net number is arithmetically correct and analytically empty.

Concentration and crowding are also distinct, and the distinction has consequences. Concentration concerns how exposure is *distributed*. Crowding concerns *similarity* in positions, assumptions, or response rules. A market can be concentrated without participants following the same strategy, or crowded across many participants with no single participant being large.

And crowding does not guarantee reversal. A crowded position can persist for a very long time while capital, performance incentives, liquidity, and information continue to support it. Its significance is that many participants may respond similarly *if* conditions change — which is a statement about sensitivity, not about timing.

Stored pressure, with limits

Positioning creates the potential for future demand: to buy, sell, hedge, rebalance, finance, roll, cover, or reduce, if relevant conditions change.

This is sometimes compared to stored potential energy, and the comparison is useful only if its limits are stated alongside it. **A market position does not contain a predetermined quantity of future movement.** Exposure does not guarantee any particular response. The analogy describes a possibility, not a mechanism with a known magnitude.

Potential adjustment becomes actual activity only when something activates it: a price threshold or drawdown limit, a change in variability or correlation, the passage of time and option expiration, funding stress or a collateral call, a risk-budget limit, a scheduled rebalancing, deteriorating liquidity, investor redemptions or inflows, or new information.

So the discipline is: positioning influences future behavior through *possible* adjustment requirements. It does not compel anything mechanically.

What can actually be observed, and how weak it is

Positioning evidence comes in classes, and the classes differ enormously in how much they can support.

Class	Examples	Principal limitation
Direct or reported	Regulatory holdings, institutional filings, futures commitment reports, short interest, exchange open interest	Often delayed, aggregated, incomplete, and unable to show related hedges
Transaction-derived	Open-interest changes, creation and redemption activity, rollover patterns	Transactions do not reveal intent or remaining economic exposure
Derivative sensitivity	How an option portfolio responds to price, volatility, and time	Model-dependent; changes with market variables; reveals no motive
Model-based estimates	Dealer exposure, trend-following exposure, volatility-control exposure, hedging demand	Depend on assumptions about ownership, strategy rules, hedging behavior, and portfolio composition
Market manifestations	Basis behavior, borrowing cost, price response near strikes, forced activity	May have several competing explanations

Every positioning claim should disclose which of these it rests on. "Positioning is stretched" built on the fourth row is a very different statement from the same words built on the first, and the sentence looks identical either way.

Two structural weaknesses are worth naming. Reported positions are not necessarily equivalent to total economic exposure. And reported exposure is not necessarily equivalent to intent. Positioning data are weakest exactly where exposures are most complex: private portfolios, cross-instrument hedges, structured products, rapidly changing dealer books, and funding relationships.

Options, sensitivity, and the dealer question

Derivatives create exposures whose sensitivity changes continuously. The contract quantity can stay identical while the economic exposure evolves.

The standard sensitivities have Greek letters attached, and the letters are less important than what they are. *Delta* describes sensitivity to a change in the underlying price. *Gamma* describes how delta itself changes as the price moves. *Vega* describes sensitivity to changes in implied volatility. *Theta* describes sensitivity to the passage of time, subject to model and convention. Others describe how these interact.

Here is the sentence that matters:

> **A Greek is a model-based sensitivity of an instrument or portfolio. It is not a trade, a participant's motive, or proof that anybody must hedge in a particular way.**

This is where a great deal of contemporary market commentary goes wrong, and it goes wrong confidently. The reasoning usually runs: dealers are estimated to hold a particular option exposure, therefore they must hedge in a particular direction, therefore a specific price move follows mechanically.

Each step in that chain hides an assumption.

Dealer-positioning estimates are conditional on things that are usually unknown: which side of each transaction the dealer took, who the customer was, what offsetting positions exist elsewhere in the book, how the firm nets exposure internally, and what its actual hedging policy is. Change any of those assumptions and the estimated exposure can invert.

The exposure estimate can also be reasonable and the behavioral conclusion still wrong. A sensitivity describes how a portfolio's value responds. It does not establish that the holder will trade, when, in what size, in which instrument, or whether they have already done so.

This does not make dealer-positioning analysis worthless. It makes it conditional. Stated carefully — *under central ownership assumptions, estimated exposure suggests greater sensitivity near current prices, though ownership, netting, and hedging policy remain uncertain* — it is legitimate evidence. Stated as a mechanism that must produce a price outcome, it is a model claim wearing an observation's clothing.

SIDEBAR

Why the Same Indicator Can Mean Different Things

Take one observation: open interest in index put options has risen substantially.

The recorded fact is that the number of outstanding contracts increased. That is all. Now consider what could produce it.

- Investors bought protection against a decline.
- Other investors sold puts to generate income.
- New spread positions were established across several strikes or expirations.
- Market makers took the other side and hold offsetting positions elsewhere.
- Futures or other options offset the apparent exposure entirely.

Each of these is consistent with the same observation. Several of them imply opposite things about who is exposed to what. And open interest, by construction, counts contracts without identifying which side holds the directional view — every contract has two sides.

So "put open interest is rising, investors are bearish" is not a compressed version of the truth. It is one of five readings, chosen because it is the easiest to narrate.

A stronger analysis looks at which strikes and expirations, at estimates of whether positions were opened or closed, at what implied volatility did at the same time, at activity in the underlying, at plausible ownership, at possible offsets — and then at how much the conclusion changes if the ownership assumption is wrong. If it changes a lot, the conclusion was never about the market. It was about the assumption.

This pattern is not specific to options. Rising volume, widening spreads, increasing short interest, and heavy futures activity all admit several readings. The discipline is the same each time: enumerate the readings before choosing one, and say which evidence would separate them.

A worked case

Suppose contract-level open interest rises at selected strikes and expirations, and the concentration of open interest increases relative to prior levels and nearby contracts.

What is recorded. Outstanding contracts increased at those strikes.

What is measured. Concentration increased relative to a stated baseline.

What this may be evidence of. Exposure has accumulated in those contracts.

What remains unknown. Which participants hold each side; whether the positions are hedged; whether they are parts of spreads; whether they are newly opened or transferred; and how any dealer involved manages the resulting inventory.

A defensible interpretation. The market may possess increased sensitivity around those strike prices, while the direction of that sensitivity and any future hedging demand remain uncertain.

What would change it. New data revealing offsets, closures, changed volatility, or different ownership.

That is the whole exercise, and the fifth step is the one that usually goes missing. The interpretation is genuinely useful. It is also considerably weaker than "the market is positioned for a decline," which is what the same data is routinely used to support.

Four stages of an exposure

Stage one: the transaction. An institution purchases one million shares. Price rises modestly; volume increases. What is established is that shares transferred from sellers to the institution.

What is not established: whether the institution will keep buying; whether the sellers were closing longs or establishing hedges; whether a dealer temporarily absorbed inventory; whether options or futures were used to offset the exposure; and whether the trade was strategic, tactical, passive, or driven by a liability.

Stage two: the resulting structure. The institution now holds a concentrated long position. A dealer may hold temporary short inventory. Derivative hedges may have been created. Gross exposure in the market has increased even if net directional exposure changed only modestly.

Stage three: prices decline. The same decline produces different responses from different participants. The long-term institution may do

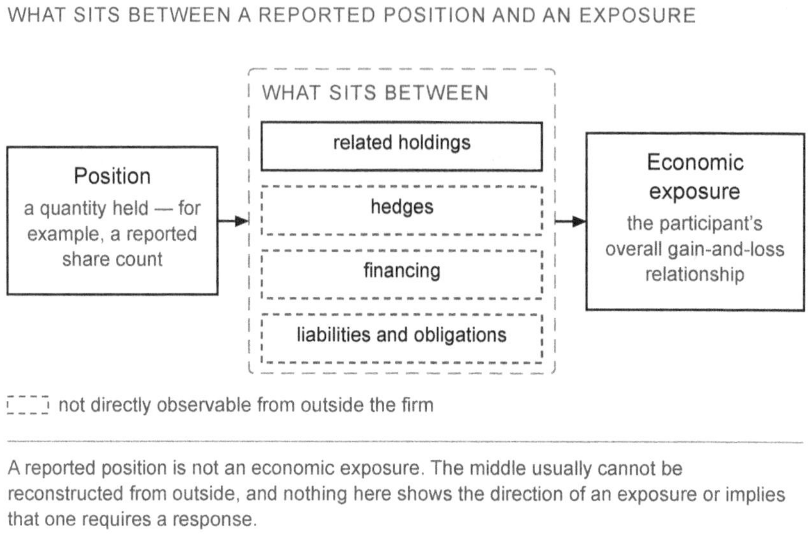

Figure 6. From a reported position to an economic exposure. The middle usually cannot be reconstructed from outside.

nothing. A leveraged fund may reduce. Dealers may hedge changing sensitivities. Short sellers may cover. Passive funds may rebalance on their own schedule. Those supplying liquidity may reduce their quoted size.

One price change; six different behaviors; no contradiction. The participants face different exposures, financing arrangements, objectives, and constraints.

Stage four: capacity thins. If many participants attempt to adjust while the capacity to absorb those adjustments is limited, price impact can stop being proportional. Variability rises. Forced execution increases. The decline can become partly self-reinforcing.

The conclusion the example supports is precise: positioning influences possible response. It does not determine market behavior on its own.

What stress reveals

Stress exposes structures that looked stable in ordinary conditions: margin calls and collateral shortages, stop-loss and drawdown rules, adjustments by strategies that target a level of variability, investor redemptions, dealer inventory limits, expiration effects, and correlated risk reduction across participants who did not know they were correlated.

The governing observation: **positioning becomes most consequential when many participants face similar adjustment pressures at a moment when the market's capacity to absorb them is insufficient.** That is a statement about the interaction of two domains, and Chapter 8 is where it is developed properly.

Common misreadings

The misreading	Why it fails
Price direction reveals positioning	Price is a transaction outcome that can arise from many mechanisms
Flow equals remaining exposure	A transaction may open, close, transfer, or hedge
Every long is a bull	Positions arise from hedging, replication, arbitrage, regulation, and facilitation
Net exposure is the whole story	Net measures conceal gross, leveraged, and offsetting exposure
Open interest is directional	It records outstanding contracts; every one has two sides
Greeks are future trades	They are model sensitivities, not obligations
Crowded positions must reverse soon	Crowding can persist while supporting conditions hold

To which add: comparing position sizes across markets without normalizing for capital, variability, liquidity, and leverage produces comparisons that mean nothing, and treating a delayed report as a description of current conditions ignores that positioning can change entirely before the report is published.

What positioning cannot tell you

Positioning analysis cannot independently establish participant intent, complete ownership across a market, hidden or offsetting exposures, future decisions, whether hedging will occur, whether any threshold will be reached, whether liquidity will remain available, future direction, fair value, how long crowding will last, or whether a model-based estimate is correctly specified.

That is a long list of things it cannot do. What remains is genuinely valuable: positioning helps explain why the same news, the same price change, or the same increase in variability can produce very different outcomes in different markets. It is a domain about *sensitivity*, and sensitivity is exactly what the price does not show you.

Takeaway

After every transaction, something remains: an exposure, a financing arrangement, a sensitivity, a distance to a limit. Positioning is the name for what remains, and it is only partially observable — reported late, aggregated, netted, or inferred through models with assumptions inside them.

It is not price, not flow, and not sentiment. Its significance comes from structure rather than size: leverage, concentration, crowding, convexity, and how close participants sit to conditions that would compel them to act.

Positioning creates the potential for future demand. Whether that potential becomes activity depends on triggers, constraints, and choices that have not happened yet. Anyone who tells you what positioning *means* the market will do next has skipped every one of those steps.

Where positioning concerns what participants are carrying, the next chapter concerns how much prices are actually moving, and what that does and does not say about what anyone is feeling.

CHAPTER SIX

Volatility: How Uncertainty Shows Up in Prices

The most measured, least understood number in markets

Volatility is quantified more precisely than almost anything else in finance and interpreted more loosely than almost anything else in public commentary. It gets described as uncertainty, as risk, as fear, as instability, and occasionally as a forecast. It is none of those things, though it is related to several of them, and the relationships are conditional.

There is a reason the confusion persists. Volatility is the domain where a genuinely technical quantity meets an intuitively emotional experience. Prices moving sharply *feels* like fear, and a number that rises when prices move sharply is easy to describe that way. The description is comfortable, and it routinely produces wrong conclusions.

This chapter keeps the statistical meaning of volatility intact and places it inside a systems context. That means being precise about what is observed, what is calculated, what is inferred through a model, and what is being assumed.

What volatility is

> **Volatility is the degree and structure of variability observed or implied in market prices, over a specified horizon and under a specified measurement method.**

Four things are packed into that.

It concerns variability, not direction. A market that falls steadily and one that rises steadily can have identical volatility.

It may be estimated from observed prices or inferred from option prices. Those are different operations producing different quantities.

Its value depends on the horizon and the method. A twenty-day estimate and a five-minute estimate are not competing answers to one question; they are answers to different questions.

It has structure. Timing, asymmetry, persistence, how variation is distributed across a market, and how components move together may matter as much as a single summary number.

Within this framework, volatility is the domain that organizes evidence about how uncertainty, sensitivity, disagreement, information processing, trading conditions, and participant adjustment become expressed through price variability and option valuations. That phrasing is careful on purpose. It does not claim uncertainty is the sole cause of variability. Prices can move because of mechanical hedging, forced liquidation, thin conditions, changing risk premia, market structure, leverage, scheduled activity, discontinuous information, or the measurement choices themselves.

Prices are observed; volatility is constructed

It is often said that volatility is observable. That statement needs care.

Transactions, quotations, closing prices, and option premiums are observed. Returns, ranges, variances, and volatility estimates are built from those observations.

Layer	What happens
Observed market data	Prices, quotes, trades, and option premiums are recorded
Constructed series	Observed prices are transformed into returns or ranges
Measurement or inference	An estimator or an option model produces a volatility value
Evidence claim	The value is evaluated against a question and a baseline
Interpretation	A qualified conclusion is drawn

A precise number does not remove measurement uncertainty. Different sampling frequencies, windows, annualization conventions, price sources, option models, and data-cleaning rules can produce materially different volatility values from the same market on the same day. All of them can be correct. They are answers to differently specified questions.

Uncertainty and volatility are not the same

This is the distinction that does the most work, and it is easiest to see through two situations.

High uncertainty, low volatility. Participants are waiting for a major policy announcement. The outcome is genuinely unknown. Trading is balanced, liquidity is deep, and many participants have reduced activity precisely because they do not know what is coming. Prices stay in a narrow range. Uncertainty is substantial; realized volatility is low.

Volatility rising as uncertainty resolves. The announcement arrives close to expectations, and one important unknown is settled. But exposure is concentrated, capacity is thin, and hedging demand accelerates. Prices move sharply. Realized volatility rises *even though* part of the original uncertainty has just been removed.

Uncertainty can exist without producing volatility, and volatility can rise as a source of uncertainty is being resolved. Anyone treating a volatility measure as a direct reading of how much is unknown will be wrong in both of those situations, which are common.

Volatility is not risk

Volatility describes variability. Risk concerns the possibility and the consequences of undesirable outcomes for a *particular* participant, portfolio, institution, or system.

Risk depends on position direction, leverage, financing, liabilities, horizon, liquidity, path, optionality, objectives, and tolerance for loss. The same volatility therefore creates different risks for different participants.

Upside variability may benefit a long option holder and harm someone who sold the option. Downside variability threatens a leveraged investor far more than an unleveraged long-term one. A stable price series may conceal credit, funding, or jump risk entirely. A small, fully funded position in a volatile instrument may carry less risk than a heavily leveraged position in a quiet one.

There is also a second-order relationship worth noting: **low realized volatility can encourage leverage that increases future fragility.** Quiet markets make larger positions look affordable. The quiet is real; the affordability may be temporary.

Not fear, not instability, not direction

	Concept	What it is
Fear	A psychological or behavioral state	Variability can rise for mechanical, informational, or liquidity reasons that involve no fear at all
Instability	Reduced resilience, fragile feedback, susceptibility to disruption	High volatility occurs in perfectly functional markets; low volatility can coexist with hidden fragility
Direction	The sign and persistence of price movement	Volatility measures variability, not whether prices rise or fall
Uncertainty	What is unknown about outcomes and mechanisms	Volatility is one possible expression of it, not the thing itself
Risk	Consequences for a particular participant or system	Risk is exposure-specific; volatility is a market measurement

A market can show high volatility with no sustained direction, high volatility inside a strong advance, low volatility during a persistent decline, or rising implied volatility before any meaningful realized movement occurs. Every one of those combinations is ordinary.

Where volatility comes from

It helps to separate what starts a movement from what determines its size.

Initiating influences include new economic, corporate, or policy information; changes in expectations; geopolitical developments; institutional rebalancing; order imbalance; changes in funding or collateral; and unexpected events.

Transmission conditions include weak or fragmented liquidity; concentrated or leveraged exposure; dealer hedging and nonlinear exposure; correlated strategies and common risk limits; margin and collateral rules; feedback trading; market closures and gaps; and changes in what participants require as compensation for bearing volatility exposure.

This is Chapter 1's argument in a specific domain. The same initiating event can produce almost nothing under one arrangement of conditions and something extraordinary under another. **Volatility cannot be understood from the event alone.**

Volatility is also consequential in its own right, not merely a response. Rising volatility can widen spreads and reduce quoted size. It can increase margin and collateral requirements. It changes option sensitivities, producing new hedging demand. Risk-control systems may reduce exposure as measured volatility rises, producing selling that increases measured volatility further. So volatility is both a response to changing conditions and a condition that changes subsequent behavior — which is why it appears on both sides of most feedback descriptions in this book.

The forms worth distinguishing

Form	What it represents	Principal limitation
Realized or historical	Variability calculated from past prices under a chosen method	Backward-looking; sensitive to window, sampling, and estimator
Implied	The volatility input that reconciles an option-pricing model with an observed option price	Model-conditioned; affected by strike, maturity, supply, demand, liquidity, and risk premia
Expected	Someone's forecast or belief about future variability	Not directly observable; may be wrong
Volatility risk premium	Compensation embedded in volatility-related prices relative to variability that is subsequently realized	Definition, horizon, and conventions vary

Two further constructions appear in professional work and are worth knowing by name: option-derived pricing of variance under a defined methodology, and volatility inferred for a future interval from the structure of prices across maturities. Both depend heavily on model and implementation choices.

Realized volatility depends on how you build it

Realized volatility is estimated from observed price changes, and the estimate is inseparable from its construction. Choices include whether returns are arithmetic or logarithmic, how frequently prices are sampled, how long the window is, whether close-to-close or intraday data are used, whether overnight movement is included, what annualization convention applies, and how missing data, closures, and outliers are treated.

A twenty-session daily estimate and a five-minute intraday estimate may both be valid while describing different aspects of the same market. **The value should never be detached from its construction.** When two sources report different volatility for the same instrument, the usual explanation is not that one is wrong. It is that they answered different questions and reported the answers with the same word.

Implied volatility

Implied volatility is inferred, not observed. It is the volatility input that causes an option-pricing model to match an observed option price, given the other inputs and assumptions: the underlying price, the strike, time to expiration, interest rates and carry, dividends where relevant, the exercise convention, the model's structure, and the quality of the price being matched.

Because it is obtained by solving a model, every assumption in that model rides inside the resulting number.

What it may reflect is a longer list than most commentary allows: expected future variability, event risk, the pricing of tail risk, demand for protection, dealer inventory, option-market liquidity, hedging pressure, and the compensation required for bearing volatility exposure. All of these can move it. None of them can be separated out from the number alone.

The governing statement:

> **Implied volatility is a model-conditioned market price of option exposure. It is not a pure or unbiased forecast of future realized volatility.**

That sentence is doing a great deal of work, and it is worth being explicit about what it rules out. It rules out reading implied volatility as "what the market expects." It rules out treating a gap between implied and subsequently realized volatility as evidence that the market was wrong. And it rules out treating an implied-volatility field delivered by a data vendor as an observation, even though it arrives looking exactly like one.

SIDEBAR

Why Implied Volatility Is Not Fear

A widely quoted volatility index is regularly called "the fear gauge." The nickname is memorable, and it obscures almost everything that matters.

What such an index actually measures is option-derived pricing of variance under a defined methodology. Someone chose which options to include, how to weight them, which maturities to interpolate between, and how to handle stale or missing quotes. The output is a construction with a specification, not a reading of a collective emotional state.

Now consider what can move it upward without anyone becoming frightened.

An earnings announcement is scheduled. Options covering that date become more expensive because the event will happen before expiration. This is arithmetic about a calendar, not sentiment.

A large institution buys protection as part of a routine risk policy, and there are fewer sellers than usual. The price of that protection rises. This is supply and demand in a specific market for a specific instrument.

Option-market liquidity thins. Wider bid-ask spreads feed into the calculation. The index rises because the inputs got noisier.

The compensation participants require for bearing volatility exposure increases. The index rises without anyone's expectation of future movement having changed at all.

And it can fall while things get worse. A market that has already declined substantially, where protection has been monetized and hedging demand has been satisfied, can show a falling volatility index while its capacity to trade remains impaired and exposure remains concentrated.

None of this means the index is uninformative. It means it measures what it measures: the price of option exposure, under a stated method, at a stated moment. Calling it fear substitutes a story about people for a fact about prices — and the story is the part you cannot check.

Term structure, skew, and what they can and cannot say

Implied volatility varies across maturities and across strike prices, and both variations get read as sentiment more often than they should.

Term structure compares implied volatility across maturities. Differences may reflect scheduled events, near-term versus long-horizon uncertainty, carry, supply and demand, expectations that variability will return toward some longer-run level, liquidity, and risk premia. When near-dated implied volatility exceeds longer-dated, that pattern may accompany acute near-term demand or stress. It does not prove panic, an imminent decline, or any particular directional outcome.

Skew describes differences in implied volatility across strike prices for the same maturity. It may reflect asymmetric demand for protection, expectations about discontinuous moves, leverage effects, dealer inventory, the supply of structured products, the pricing of severe outcomes, model limitations, or liquidity differences between strikes. Skew is not a direct measure of sentiment and does not reveal intent on its own. Its meaning depends on the maturity, how far the strike sits from the current price, option liquidity, the timing of scheduled events, and comparison against an appropriate baseline.

Structure that a single number hides

Several properties of volatility are well established and are worth carrying.

Clustering. Large movements tend to occur near other large movements, and quiet periods tend to persist. Volatility is not independent through time.

Asymmetry. Volatility may respond differently to declines than to advances. Several mechanisms have been proposed; the observed pattern does not by itself establish which one is operating.

Jumps. Prices can change discontinuously rather than through small continuous steps. Models built on continuous movement will understate this.

Fat tails. Extreme returns occur more often than simple normal models imply. Tail risk cannot be inferred reliably from a standard deviation.

Horizon dependence. Short- and long-horizon measures convey different information, so comparisons require matched horizons.

Dispersion and correlation. Aggregate volatility does not reveal how movement is distributed. Individual instruments may move a great deal while an index stays moderate, if they are not moving together. An index can become far more volatile because correlations converged, without any component becoming more volatile. Calm at the index level can conceal substantial variation underneath it.

That last point is a specific instance of a general one: a stable average can coexist with unstable components.

From an observation to a conclusion

Suppose near-term implied volatility rises ahead of a company's earnings announcement.

What is recorded. Option prices rose relative to the current underlying price and other model inputs.

What is measured. Near-term implied volatility increased, possibly with changes in skew and term structure.

What this may be evidence of. The market is pricing greater near-term variability, or greater compensation for bearing volatility exposure.

Alternative explanations. Reduced option liquidity; one-sided demand; dealer inventory; event hedging; an error in a model input; a wider volatility risk premium.

A defensible interpretation. Uncertainty or demand for protection may have increased. The observation does not determine price direction and does not guarantee that realized volatility will exceed implied volatility.

What would change it. Option liquidity normalizing; the event passing; realized movement differing materially; new information revealing a different mechanism.

Three sessions

Session A. The index trades in a narrow intraday range. Spreads stay narrow, depth is stable, realized intraday volatility is low, implied volatility barely moves, and participation is balanced.

Session B. The index finishes with the same net return as Session A. But the intraday range is much larger. Prices reverse repeatedly. Spreads widen, depth declines, implied volatility and skew rise, and hedging activity accelerates.

The closing number is identical. The path, and the condition of the market that produced it, are entirely different. Anyone comparing only closing prices would record these as the same day.

Session C. The index moves steadily in one direction. Liquidity stays functional. Pullbacks are limited. Implied volatility is stable or falling. Participation is broad. The total return is larger than in either A or B, and the path is orderly.

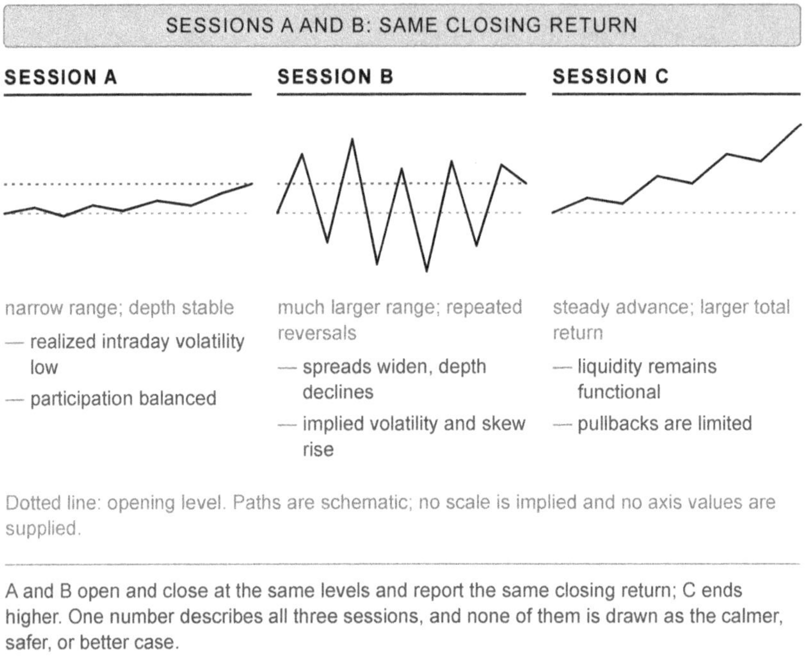

Figure 7. Sessions A and B report the same closing return. A closing return does not describe a session.

The lesson runs in both directions. A large return does not imply disorderly volatility, and a small closing return does not imply a calm market.

What stress looks like here

Stress in this domain may involve rapid expansion in realized volatility; jumps and price gaps; steepening skew; near-dated implied volatility exceeding longer-dated; rising variability *of* volatility itself; correlations converging upward; widening option spreads; reduced executable liquidity; and higher margin and collateral requirements.

No single one of those proves systemic stress. Any of them can appear in an ordinary market for ordinary reasons. Assessment requires evidence across domains, explicit attention to data quality and horizon, and consideration of alternative explanations — which is the argument of Chapter 8, arriving here in its most concrete form.

Common misreadings

The misreading	Why it fails
Volatility is uncertainty	Uncertainty can be high while variability is low, and volatility can rise as uncertainty resolves
Volatility is risk	Risk depends on the participant's exposure, leverage, horizon, and consequences
Volatility is fear	Variability arises from mechanical, informational, and liquidity mechanisms too
Low volatility means safety	Low measured variability can conceal leverage, jump, credit, and funding risk
Implied volatility is a forecast	It is model-conditioned and includes supply, demand, liquidity, and risk premia
A volatility index is a fear gauge	It measures option-derived variance pricing under a defined methodology
Realized and implied are interchangeable	One is estimated from past prices; the other is inferred from option prices
Annualized volatility is a one-year forecast	Annualization is a scaling convention, not a prediction

Three more, briefly. Comparing volatility figures with different horizons, sampling intervals, or estimators compares answers to different questions. Ignoring skew and term structure discards most of the available information in favor of a single at-the-money number. And treating estimated option-related exposure as if it dictates flow converts a model sensitivity into a forecast, as Chapter 5 discussed.

What volatility cannot tell you

Volatility analysis cannot independently establish future direction, fair value, participant intent, the complete cause of variability, whether uncertainty is rising or falling, whether implied volatility is expensive or cheap, whether realized volatility will match implied, whether a market is stable or fragile, whether liquidity will remain available, whether a pattern will persist, or whether a model is correctly specified.

Volatility measurements are conditional representations. Their usefulness depends on the question being asked, the horizon, the estimator, the data quality, and the other conditions they are read alongside.

Takeaway

Volatility describes how much and in what pattern prices move, over a stated horizon, by a stated method. It is not uncertainty, not risk, not fear, not instability, and not direction, though it is entangled with several of them in ways that depend on circumstances.

Prices are observed. Realized volatility is calculated. Implied volatility is inferred through a model and carries that model's assumptions inside it. Expected future volatility is nobody's observation at all.

The domain is most informative when read alongside the others: the same volatility means something different in a market with deep capacity and dispersed exposure than in one with thin capacity and concentrated exposure. What it never does on its own is reveal cause, intent, value, direction, or outcome.

The next chapter takes up the most visible of the four domains and the one most often mistaken for an explanation.

CHAPTER SEVEN

Trend: When Direction Persists

What "the trend is up" actually claims

It is the most common sentence in market commentary and one of the least specified. Up over what period? Measured how? For which instrument, and against what? Up for the index, or for the securities inside it? Up in a way that would still be called up if you moved the starting date by two weeks?

Trend is the most visible of the four domains. Anyone can see a chart rising. It is also the least self-explanatory, because what people see on a chart is a price history, and what they mean by "trend" is a claim about persistence that requires a method to establish and a horizon to be true of.

There is a further problem. Trend is routinely treated as though it were a force acting on the market — something that carries prices along and can be relied on until it "breaks." A systems view requires more care. Prices are observed. Persistence is inferred, from a sequence of observations, using rules that somebody chose.

What trend is

Trend is sustained directional persistence in a market variable, over a specified horizon, identified through a stated measurement method, and interpreted within the surrounding conditions.

Within this framework, trend is treated as an *emergent* directional condition, produced and modified through interactions among information, liquidity, positioning, volatility, participant behavior, and time. It is not an independent cause.

Trend exists in degrees. It does not require uninterrupted movement and can coexist with pullbacks, gaps, and temporary counter-movement. Its classification depends on scale, method, and the purpose of the analysis.

Although price is the usual subject, other variables trend too: volatility, spreads, yields, volume, breadth, and measures of positioning can all show directional persistence.

Movement is not trend

Every transaction can change a price. Not every price change produces persistence. Three cases make the difference concrete.

Isolated movement. A security trades at 100. A large order pushes it to 101, and it returns to 100 shortly afterward. Movement happened. Persistence did not.

A retained level shift. The security moves from 100 to 101 and stays near the new level. The market may have accepted a step change. A continuing trend has not been established.

A persistent advance. The security moves from 100 to 101 to 102 to 103 across multiple observations, retaining each move after pullbacks, with participation broadening. Evidence of trend becomes stronger.

The principle: **magnitude alone does not establish trend.** A single large jump produces a large return without producing persistence. Persistence and path are what distinguish trend from movement.

Prices are observed; trend is classified

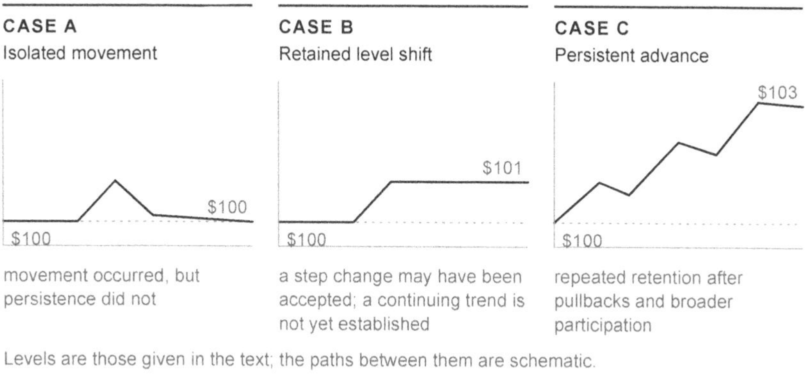

Figure 8. Isolated movement, a retained level shift, and a persistent advance. Magnitude alone does not establish a trend.

	Layer
Observed data	Prices, returns, volume, and related data are recorded
Directional features	Returns, slopes, highs and lows, or other measures are constructed
Persistence measurement	The continuity, duration, or consistency of direction is assessed
Classification	A rule or model assigns a label
Structural interpretation	Breadth, leadership, liquidity, volatility, and positioning are evaluated

Trend rules can use moving-average relationships, slope thresholds, cumulative returns, sequences of highs and lows, whether breakouts are retained, persistence scores, filters, or statistical regime models.

Here is the part that matters: **different defensible methods may classify the same period differently.** Two competent analysts can disagree about whether a market is trending without either of them making an error, because they applied different rules. When someone says the trend is up, the honest follow-up question is not "are you sure?" It is "by what method, over what horizon?"

A trend statement that means something

A market may rise over several months, decline over several days, and go nowhere over several hours. All three descriptions can be simultaneously correct, because market behavior is nested across horizons.

A complete trend statement identifies the instrument or market, the variable being evaluated, the direction, the horizon, the measurement method, the breadth of participation, and the relevant qualification.

Compare two statements about the same market.

> The market is bullish.

> The capitalization-weighted index maintained positive twelve-week price persistence, while five-session momentum, equal-weight participation, and small-capitalization relative strength all weakened.

The second is longer, and it is checkable, falsifiable, and considerably more useful. It also happens to contain a warning that the first conceals entirely.

Five words that are not synonyms

	Term
Direction	The sign of movement over an interval
Return	The magnitude of gain or loss over an interval
Trend	Persistence of direction across multiple observations or a defined horizon
Momentum	Recent directional strength or return persistence, under a stated method
Acceleration	A change in the rate or strength of movement, under a stated measure

Momentum has several established meanings in finance: recent return, persistence through time, relative performance against peers, or a ranked strategy across a cross-section. The method has to be stated, because they do not mean the same thing.

The distinction between trend and momentum is best seen in a sequence.

Week	Closing price	Change
1	100	—
2	104	+4
3	107	+3
4	109	+2
5	110	+1

Price rises every week, so upward direction persists. The weekly gain declines every week, so recent directional strength is weakening. **The trend may remain intact while momentum slows**, and these are frequently reported as though they were the same observation moving in opposite directions.

Note also what this sequence does not establish: nothing here says whether week six is higher or lower. Slowing momentum is compatible with continued advance at a reduced pace, with a pause, and with a reversal.

Trend has no single cause

Persistent direction can arise through several pathways, and which one is operating changes what the trend implies.

Pathway	Illustrative mechanism
Information-led	New information changes expectations, producing sustained demand or supply
Liquidity-led	Withdrawal of bids or offers allows one-sided movement to persist
Positioning-led	Short covering, liquidation, or rebalancing produces repeated directional flow
Hedging-led	Derivative sensitivities generate recurring buying or selling
Allocation-led	Gradual institutional, systematic, or passive capital movement sustains direction
Feedback-led	Performance, narratives, risk capacity, and trend-following behavior reinforce persistence

The information-to-buying story is the one everyone reaches for, and it is only one of six. Markets can trend without any discrete information event, through slow allocation, mechanical rebalancing, thinning liquidity, or transmission from another market.

This matters because the pathways have different implications. A trend sustained by broad reassessment of value behaves differently from one sustained by participants closing positions they cannot afford to hold, even though both look identical on a price chart.

Who is participating

An index can rise while most of its components fall, because index weights are usually uneven. Breadth describes how widely directional behavior is distributed across a defined universe.

It can be assessed through advancing versus declining securities, the percentage above selected reference levels, new highs against new lows, equal-weighted versus capitalization-weighted performance, sector participation, volume breadth, how concentrated the contribution to the total return is, and how widely returns are dispersed across the cross-section.

Every one of those depends on the universe definition, index membership, weighting, threshold, horizon, and data treatment. A broadly supported advance has a different structure from a narrowly supported one.

But here is the qualification that most breadth commentary drops: **breadth describes how widely directional behavior is distributed; it does not independently determine whether the trend will continue.** Narrow advances can persist for a long time. Broad advances can reverse. Breadth is structural evidence about the character of a move, not a timing indication about its end.

Leadership is the related question of *which* securities, sectors, or factors are driving the movement, and rotation is the question of how that changes. Leadership analysis asks which groups lead, relative to what benchmark, for how long, with what breadth and liquidity, whether leadership is broadening, rotating, narrowing, or weakening, and whether the leaders account for an increasing share of the total return. It is observational evidence about where capital and attention are moving. It does not prove causation or continuation.

Strength, structure, and quality

Three different questions get compressed into "how strong is this trend?"

Dimension	The question	Evidence
Strength	How large, steep, or persistent is the movement?	Slope, cumulative return, persistence, time above reference levels, drawdown behavior
Structure	What conditions accompany and sustain the direction?	Breadth, leadership, liquidity, volatility, positioning, cross-asset consistency, path
Quality	A summary assessment of the observed structure	An interpretation, not a guarantee

The third row needs its warning attached. **Trend quality is an interpretive assessment of the conditions accompanying directional movement. It is not a measure of durability or desirability.** A trend can have excellent structure and end tomorrow for reasons nothing in its structure anticipated.

Trends change the conditions that produced them

Persistent direction alters participant behavior, and the alteration works in both directions.

Some feedback reinforces: momentum-oriented participation, short covering, performance chasing, systematic allocation, improving collateral and risk capacity, and narrative reinforcement.

Some feedback limits: valuation constraints, position crowding, risk limits, liquidity exhaustion, profit taking, adverse information, and rising volatility.

The important qualification is that these are not sequential phases. **Feedback may extend a trend, and the same feedback may increase fragility** by concentrating exposure and reducing the pool of participants who have not yet acted. A trend can become stronger and more vulnerable at the same time, which is Chapter 8's territory and one of the more counterintuitive ideas in this book.

From an indicator to a claim

Consider the most widely used trend observation there is: price is above a rising fifty-day moving average.

What is recorded. Daily closing prices for a specified instrument.

What is measured. Price is above the fifty-day average, and the average has a positive slope.

What this may be evidence of. Medium-horizon upward directional persistence, *under the selected parameterization.*

Alternative explanations. A recent price gap doing most of the work; narrow leadership; temporary liquidity effects; sensitivity to the parameter choice; survivorship in the sample being examined.

A defensible interpretation. An upward trend may be present under the selected method. Breadth, stability, and durability require additional evidence.

What would change it. Price repeatedly failing to retain the structure; the slope changing materially; alternative measures providing stronger contrary evidence.

The phrase doing the most work is *under the selected parameterization.* Fifty days is a convention. Forty and sixty are equally defensible and will sometimes disagree. **Parameter choices are design decisions, not properties of the market**, and a classification that flips when the window changes by ten percent was never describing something robust.

Same return, different market

Market A. An index rises 10% over four months. Participation is broad. Liquidity stays stable. Volatility is moderate. Pullbacks are absorbed in an orderly way. Leadership rotates among several sectors. Exposure expands gradually.

Market B. The index also rises 10% over four months. A few large securities drive most of the gain. Liquidity deteriorates specifically during declines. Volatility rises as prices advance. Leadership narrows continuously. Exposure becomes increasingly concentrated.

The return is identical. The underlying conditions are not. Market A can be described as broadly supported. Market B is directionally strong and increasingly sensitive to disruption.

Neither description predicts what happens next. What they do is distinguish two situations that a return figure reports as the same.

A longer look at one advance

Consider a hypothetical broad equity index that advances from 5,000 to 5,400 over eight weeks — an 8% gain, with directional persistence present over the selected eight-week horizon.

Breadth. In the first four weeks, 75% of constituents trade above their intermediate reference levels. By the eighth week, only 48% do. The index continues upward while participation narrows.

Leadership. Early in the advance, industrial, financial, technology, and consumer groups all participate. Later, a small group of large technology companies accounts for most of the aggregate gain.

Liquidity. Spreads remain normal during advances but widen materially during brief declines. The market absorbs buying more readily than selling.

Positioning. Option prices and available positioning evidence are consistent with increasing upside exposure and concentrated risk in the leading securities. Who holds it, and how they will hedge, remain uncertain.

Volatility. Index realized volatility stays moderate while implied volatility for several leading stocks rises. That may reflect event risk, protection demand, option-market conditions, or increased pricing of future variability. It does not directly establish that uncertainty increased.

The interpretation. The upward price trend remains intact under the selected horizon and method. Breadth has narrowed, leadership has concentrated, downside liquidity has weakened, and exposure appears increasingly concentrated. These conditions may increase sensitivity to adverse information. They do not determine whether or when a reversal will occur.

That final sentence is not hedging. It is the accurate boundary of what the evidence supports, and every word of the assessment before it is checkable.

Deterioration, transition, failure, reversal

Four terms get used interchangeably and mean different things. A fifth is different again.

Condition	What it means	What it does not prove
Deterioration	Supporting evidence weakens while the direction persists	That reversal is imminent
Transition	Directional organization changes; persistence weakens or becomes ambiguous	That a new sustained direction exists
Failure	A breakout or continuation attempt does not retain its structure	That the opposite direction must follow
Reversal	A new sustained direction becomes established	That it will persist indefinitely
Market-state transition	The broader arrangement across all four domains changes	That price direction must reverse at the same time

The last row is the one to hold onto, and Chapter 10 develops it. **A trend transition is not the same as a market-state transition.** A market's overall arrangement can change before price direction turns, and directional structure can change while the broader system stays within the same classification.

These conditions also do not form a fixed sequence. Deterioration does not reliably lead to transition, transition does not reliably lead to failure, and failure does not reliably lead to reversal. Markets stabilize, resume, and reconfigure in several ways.

Related markets

Markets connected by ownership, funding, or economics may move consistently, diverge, lead, lag, or reflect genuinely different horizons and constraints. Equities may rise while credit spreads widen. Large-capitalization indexes may rise while smaller companies weaken.

Consistency across related markets can strengthen an interpretation. Divergence may reveal fragility, timing differences, or a legitimate structural distinction. **Divergence is evidence requiring explanation, not automatic proof of reversal**, and treating every divergence as a warning produces a great many warnings that never arrive.

Common misreadings

	The misreading
Any price movement is a trend	Movement can be isolated and non-persistent
A large return proves a trend	A single jump produces return without persistence
Slowing momentum confirms reversal	Direction may continue at a slower rate
Narrowing breadth is a sell indication	Narrow trends can persist for a long time
Broad participation guarantees continuation	Broad trends reverse too
One indicator defines the trend	Indicators are measurement methods, not the phenomenon
Moving-average parameters are objective	Parameter choices materially affect classification
Technical patterns explain cause	Patterns describe behavior; they do not explain it

Two more deserve their own mention. Classifying past trends from a completed chart makes real-time identification look far easier than it is. And a historical signal that ignores transaction costs and implementation delay may not survive contact with actual execution.

Trend is retrospective, and that is not a flaw

There is an unavoidable limitation in this domain: **persistence can only be identified after observations accumulate.** By the time enough evidence exists to classify a trend confidently, some of the movement being classified has already happened.

This is not a defect in the method. It is a property of the thing being measured. Persistence is a statement about a sequence, and a sequence has to occur before it can be assessed. Any method that identifies trends earlier does so by requiring less evidence, which is a real trade-off rather than an improvement — the same trade-off, in a different form, that Chapter 10 examines when it asks how quickly a genuine change can be confirmed.

Takeaway

Trend is persistence of direction, established by a method, over a horizon, within a set of surrounding conditions. It is not the same as movement, not the same as return, not the same as momentum, and not a force that acts on prices.

It emerges through several possible pathways, and which one is operating changes what it implies. Its structure — how broadly distributed, how concentrated the leadership, how the market behaves on declines — tells you more than its slope. And the same feedback that extends a trend can concentrate the exposure that makes it fragile.

What trend establishes is where a market variable has been going. Liquidity, positioning, and volatility help explain how that movement is being sustained and where sensitivity may be building. Which is the subject of the next chapter, and the point at which the four stop being four.

CHAPTER EIGHT

Putting the Four Together

One number, two markets

A broad equity index rises 1.5% in a session. Here are two markets in which that happened.

In the first, capacity to trade stayed deep and replenished after every transaction. Participation was broad. Price variability stayed proportionate to the movement. Exposure expanded gradually. Pullbacks during the session were absorbed efficiently.

In the second, capacity was thin and asymmetric — better on the way up than on the way down. A handful of large securities produced most of the move. Short exposure was being reduced under pressure. Implied volatility rose while prices rose. Depth on the downside replenished poorly whenever it was consumed.

The return is identical. A performance table records these as the same session. Everything else about them differs.

This chapter is about that difference, and about the fact that it cannot be seen from any one of the four domains. Liquidity alone does not show it. Positioning alone does not show it. Volatility and trend alone do not show it. It appears only in how they are arranged relative to one another.

The word we have been avoiding

We now need a term for that arrangement, and it needs to be introduced carefully because it will be distinguished from something else in the next chapter.

> **A market configuration is the detailed arrangement of observed and inferred conditions across domains, at a specified time and scale.**

Configuration preserves detail. It is not a label, not a score, and not a summary. When you say that a market has a positive intermediate trend, narrowing breadth, concentrated exposure, contained realized volatility, rising short-dated implied volatility, and downside depth that replenishes slowly — that whole statement, with all six of its parts intact, is a description of a configuration.

Up to this point the book has used ordinary phrases like "the arrangement of conditions" and "how a market is put together." Those phrases were placeholders for this one. From here on the term is *configuration*, and the reason for the precision becomes clear in Chapter 9, where configurations get compressed into something considerably smaller.

The ladder from Chapter 2 now has its middle rungs filled in:

Market phenomena → recorded data → controlled measurements → contextual evidence → domain assessments → **market configuration** → state representation.

Every step of that ladder loses something. Recorded data lose the phenomenon. Measurements lose the record's context. Evidence requires a question that not everyone will share. Domain assessments compress across measurements. Configuration is where the most detail still exists, which is why it is worth having a name for.

Measurements do not become understanding merely by being collected together. Putting a spread, an open-interest figure, an implied-volatility reading, and a moving-average slope on the same screen produces four numbers on a screen. Synthesis requires attention to what each one means, at what scale, with what data quality, over what time, in what relation to the others, and against what alternative explanations.

Four rules for reading across domains

Interactions are conditional, not universal. Weak liquidity does not always amplify volatility. Concentrated exposure does not always produce forced selling. The relationships hold under conditions, and the conditions are part of the claim.

Relationships run both ways. Volatility affects liquidity, and liquidity affects volatility. Positioning affects prices, and prices affect positioning. Circular influence is normal here, which means "X drove Y" is usually an incomplete description of something reciprocal.

Moving together does not identify causation. Several domains may change at once because they share underlying data, because they respond to the same event, or because one mechanism links them. Co-movement narrows the field of explanations. It does not select one.

Effects depend on horizon, scale, timing, thresholds, and adaptation. A relationship that holds over a session may not hold over a quarter, and a relationship that held last year may have been arbitraged away.

How the four touch each other

Liquidity and positioning. Liquidity conditions influence the cost, immediacy, depth, and price impact of establishing, adjusting, hedging, or exiting exposure. Positioning creates *potential* future demand for liquidity, depending on price movement, constraints, leverage, hedging policy, and participant choice.

Two arrangements make the interaction visible. When exposure is dispersed and capacity is deep, adjustment can occur without disproportionate disruption; that increases the market's ability to adapt without guaranteeing anything. When many participants may need to adjust similar exposure while counterparties are limited, a small disturbance can produce large price impact. Concentration alone does not cause the move, and thin capacity alone does not determine direction. The sensitivity emerges from their combination.

Liquidity and volatility. Reduced executable capacity increases price impact for a given amount of order flow. Larger price changes raise measured variability. Higher measured volatility can tighten risk limits and cause those supplying capacity to widen spreads or reduce size, which reduces capacity further. Five steps, and the loop closes.

That loop is real and it is also not the only pathway available. Wider spreads attract counterparties who were previously uninterested. Price deviations invite participants seeking value. Depth replenishes. Volatility

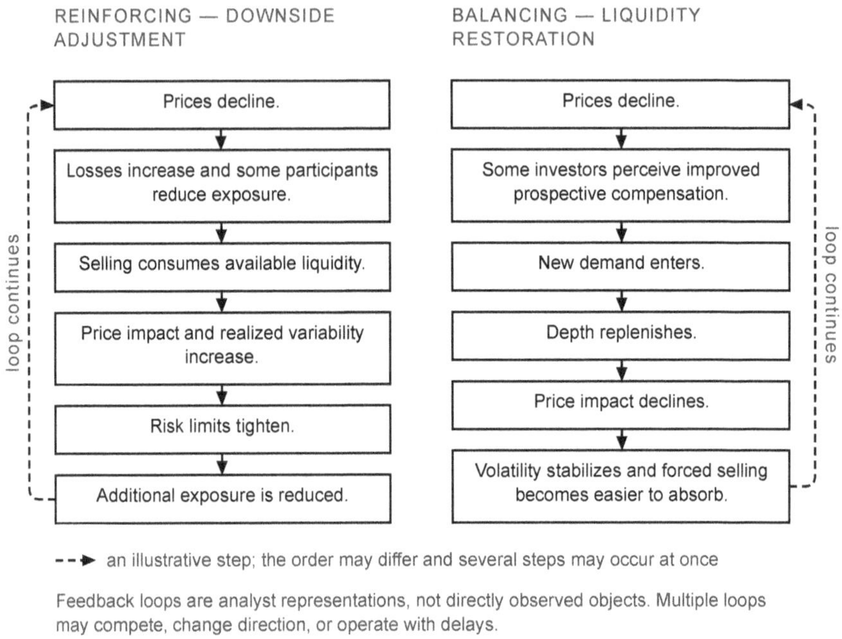

Figure 9. A reinforcing loop and a balancing loop, drawn at equal weight. Both are analysts' representations, not observed objects.

can stay high while the market's ability to function improves. **A description of the first loop without the second is not a simplification. It is a bias toward catastrophe.**

Liquidity and trend. Trend identifies sustained direction; liquidity describes how efficiently the market travels in that direction. An orderly advance may involve repeated replenishment of offers as they are consumed. A squeeze may involve withdrawal of supply and discontinuous movement. Both produce rising prices with different structures underneath. Thin conditions can exaggerate apparent trend strength, and persistent direction does not by itself establish that the market is resilient.

Positioning and volatility. Exposure creates sensitivities that may become active as prices, volatility, time, and constraints change. Consider a case where investors have purchased protective put options and dealers hold the corresponding short optionality. *If* those dealers hedge dynamically, *if* they have no offsetting exposure elsewhere, and *if* liquidity is limited, then a market decline may require additional selling from them.

Three conditionals, and they travel with the example permanently. None of them should be assumed without evidence, and all three are frequently unknown from outside the firm. What the case establishes is a possible pathway. What it does not establish is that the pathway is active.

Positioning and trend. Persistent direction changes gains, losses, risk capacity, benchmark pressure, and incentives. Systematic strategies may increase exposure. Participants positioned against the move may reduce. Profitable positions gain the capacity to expand.

Continuation can therefore increase concentration. A trend may become stronger while the configuration becomes more sensitive to disruption. Crowding is structural evidence about what could happen if conditions change; it is not a statement about when.

Volatility and trend. These are not opposites, and the combinations are all ordinary.

Trend	Volatility	Possible readings
Rising	Low and stable	Orderly persistence, muted variability, or latent leverage
Rising	Expanding	Rapid repricing, speculation, event response, or unstable participation
Declining	Expanding	Stress, forced adjustment, information shock, or disorderly repricing
Declining	Falling	Controlled weakness, drift, or reduced participation

Each cell holds several readings. This is a table for generating questions, not for producing answers.

Beyond pairs

Pairwise analysis is a teaching device. Real markets involve all four domains interacting simultaneously, alongside information, valuation, policy, technology, and participant adaptation that none of the four fully captures.

A multidomain sequence might involve concentrated exposure, then adverse movement, then rising adjustment demand, then declining capacity, then greater price impact, then expanding volatility, then trend deterioration, then further repositioning. The order can differ. Several steps can occur at once. Balancing forces can interrupt at any point.

And the sequence is a representation. Feedback loops are analysts' descriptions of interaction, not objects anyone observes directly. Drawing one does not establish that it is operating.

SIDEBAR

Six Words That Are Not Synonyms

Market commentary uses these interchangeably. They answer different questions, and being able to hold them apart is one of the most practical upgrades this book offers.

Strength — the magnitude, persistence, or intensity of an observed condition. *How strong is it?*

Stability — the degree to which organization is maintained under ordinary variation. *Does the arrangement hold together?*

Resilience — the capacity to absorb disturbance, keep functioning, and recover or reorganize. *Can it adapt without disproportionate impairment?*

Fragility — sensitivity arising from limited adaptive capacity, concentration, leverage, thin capacity, or nonlinear exposure. *How vulnerable is it to disturbance?*

Stress — observable strain: forced adjustment, impaired exchange, reduced resilience. *What strain is actually present?*

Failure — a material breakdown in a market function, mechanism, or institution. *Has something stopped working?*

Now the combinations, all of which occur.

A market can be **strong but fragile**: a powerful advance sustained by a narrowing group of participants, financed with increasing leverage.

A market can be **volatile but resilient**: prices moving sharply while transactions continue, spreads widen proportionately, depth replenishes, and price discovery stays two-sided.

A market can be **calm but adjustment-sensitive**: low measured variability concealing exposure that would require a great deal of trading if conditions changed.

A market can be **stressed while continuing to function**, which is the ordinary case and is routinely reported as breakdown.

The reason these get conflated is that only one of the six — stress — is directly observable while it is happening. Strength is measurable after the fact. Stability, resilience, and fragility are inferred. Failure is obvious only in retrospect. Every time one of the inferred ones is stated as an observation, a model output has been promoted to a fact.

Calm does not prove resilience

A market can show low realized volatility, narrow trading ranges, and a persistent advance while leverage accumulates, exposure concentrates, leadership narrows, depth weakens, and volatility-sensitive positions build up.

That combination may be consistent with increasing fragility. What it does not establish is that an abrupt change is inevitable. Fragile arrangements can persist for a very long time — longer than anyone pointing at them expects, which is why identifying fragility is so much easier than acting on it.

And volatility does not prove breakdown

The reverse case matters just as much, and gets far less attention.

After a major policy announcement, prices may move sharply while transactions continue to occur, spreads widen roughly in proportion to the movement, depth replenishes after being consumed, clearing and settlement function normally, and price discovery remains two-sided.

That market is stressed and resilient. The magnitude of movement is not the diagnostic. **The quality of adjustment is.** A large move in a functioning market and a small move in an impaired one are different events, and only the second is a problem.

The same outcome from different mechanisms

Suppose an index declines 5% over one week. At least four distinct pathways produce that number.

Path	Mechanism	Configuration
Revaluation	New information reduces expected cash flows	Orderly adjustment, functional liquidity, moderate volatility expansion
Forced deleveraging	Losses trigger risk limits and simultaneous selling	Concentrated adjustment demand, weak capacity, rapid volatility expansion
Policy uncertainty	Participants reduce activity because valuation becomes less reliable	Lower participation, thinner capacity, large movement from modest flow
Liquidity discontinuity	Bids withdraw, or access becomes limited	Discontinuous movement disproportionate to ordinary volume

Outcome does not identify mechanism. The 5% is identical in all four. What distinguishes them is the configuration, and a description that reports only the outcome has thrown away the information that mattered.

The reverse holds too. Two markets can begin with concentrated long exposure, low volatility, and a mature advance. After the same adverse event, one stays contained because demand and capacity persist. The other accelerates because those supplying capacity withdraw, leverage constraints activate, and volatility-sensitive strategies reduce exposure. Initial conditions matter, and adaptation, institutional constraints, timing, and threshold effects shape the path. Markets carry their history.

Configuration dependence

The general form of the argument now has a name.

> **Configuration dependence** means that the effect of information, order flow, or disturbance depends on the market configuration in which it occurs.

A modest earnings disappointment may produce almost nothing in a deeply liquid, lightly positioned market and something substantial in a crowded, thin one. This is the same claim Chapter 1 made about two markets and one announcement, now stated in terms the rest of the book can use.

Part of why the dependence is so strong is that market responses are frequently **nonlinear**. A change may produce little visible effect until a threshold is crossed, after which response increases rapidly. Thresholds include order-book depth depletion, margin or collateral breaches, stop-order activation, and risk limits at firms supplying capacity. Those thresholds are often unknown from outside, may change, are distributed across many institutions, and activate at different times. A disturbance twice as large does not necessarily produce twice the effect, in either direction.

Evidence from different clocks

One practical complication deserves its own note, because it quietly corrupts a great deal of multidomain analysis.

Liquidity can deteriorate within seconds. Intraday volatility changes within minutes. Reported institutional holdings may update quarterly. A long-horizon trend classification may take weeks to change.

Assembling those four into one picture means combining evidence recorded at wildly different frequencies, with different publication delays, different observation windows, and different degrees of staleness. **Evidence from different horizons may coexist, but it should not be treated as temporally equivalent.** A positioning figure published six weeks ago and a spread measured four seconds ago are not two observations of the same moment.

Building an assessment

The practical version of this chapter is four questions, asked together.

Domain	The question	Evidence
Liquidity	What capacity appears available, for what size, urgency, venue, side, and horizon?	Spreads, depth, price impact, execution quality, replenishment
Positioning	What exposure, sensitivity, leverage, concentration, and adjustment requirements are evident or inferred?	Open interest, leverage, reported holdings, short interest, estimated sensitivities
Volatility	What degree and structure of variability is realized or implied, over what horizon and by what method?	Realized and implied volatility, skew, term structure, ranges
Trend	What directional persistence is present, under what method, with what breadth and structure?	Slope, returns, persistence, breadth, leadership, cross-asset consistency

And then the question that makes it multidomain rather than four separate answers: **how do these conditions interact, and what alternative explanations remain?**

It helps to have a rough sense of what more adaptive and more sensitive configurations look like.

Domain	More adaptive	Mixed	More adjustment-sensitive
Liquidity	Deep, replenishing, resilient	Uneven or normal	Thin, asymmetric, deteriorating
Positioning	Dispersed, lower leverage, adaptable	Unclear or balanced	Concentrated, leveraged, nonlinear
Volatility	Proportionate and structurally stable	Transitional or mixed	Rapidly expanding, dislocated, unstable
Trend	Persistent, broad, orderly	Range-bound or mixed	Narrowing, deteriorating, disorderly

This matrix is a reasoning aid, not a signal. Conditions must not be counted mechanically. Three mild observations in the middle column do not offset one severe impairment in the right-hand column, and nothing about the layout implies that four "more adaptive" readings mean anything will happen or not happen. It is a prompt for asking whether you have looked at all four, and nothing more than that.

What a disciplined assessment sounds like

Here is a weak one, of a kind published every day:

> The market is bullish because price is above the fifty-day moving average and volatility is low.

And here is the same market described properly:

> The intermediate price trend remains upward under the selected method. Realized volatility remains contained, and observed liquidity appears adequate for ordinary transaction sizes. However, breadth has narrowed, exposure appears increasingly concentrated among a small group of leaders, and downside depth has replenished less effectively during recent pullbacks. The current configuration is therefore directionally persistent but less broadly supported and potentially more

adjustment-sensitive than earlier in the advance. This assessment does not determine whether or when a reversal will occur.

The second is four times longer and contains roughly twenty times as much information. Every clause is checkable. It names its method, states its qualifications, distinguishes what is observed from what is inferred, and stops exactly where the evidence stops.

A full worked assessment

At 10:30 in the morning, a broad equity index is down 0.8%. The question is whether this reflects ordinary weakness or developing short-horizon stress.

Price and trend. The index is down 0.8% from the prior close. Under the selected method, price remains above its intermediate reference level, short-horizon momentum is negative, and 70% of components are declining. This supports short-horizon deterioration inside an intermediate upward trend.

Liquidity. Spreads have widened modestly. Depth near the best prices is 25% below the normal range for this time of day. Comparable orders are moving price further than usual. Order books continue to recover after transactions. Capacity has weakened but remains functional.

Positioning. Put open interest is elevated near current prices. Estimates of dealer exposure suggest greater downside sensitivity under the central ownership assumptions. The open-interest data are delayed, and the exposure estimate is model-dependent.

Volatility. Realized intraday variability is rising. Short-dated implied volatility and downside skew have increased, while longer-dated implied volatility is comparatively stable. The options market is pricing greater near-term variability, protection demand, event risk, or risk compensation. The measurement does not establish that anyone is frightened.

Data quality. Quote data are current. One options feed had a brief gap. Dealer estimates are model-dependent. Open-interest data reflect the prior reporting update. This evidence does not deserve equal weight, and saying so is part of the assessment rather than a caveat attached to it.

The multidomain reading. The market is experiencing broad short-horizon selling within an intermediate upward price trend under the selected method. Liquidity measurements have deteriorated relative to the normal range for this time of day but remain functional. Realized intraday variability, short-dated implied volatility, and downside skew have all increased. Model-dependent positioning estimates suggest possible additional downside sensitivity, though confidence there is limited by ownership assumptions and delayed data. The configuration is consistent with developing short-horizon stress. It is not evidence of established market dysfunction.

Notice the fifth step. Most published market analysis has no equivalent of it, and its absence is why so much analysis cannot be evaluated: without knowing which inputs were current, complete, and directly observed, a reader has no way to tell how much the conclusion should be trusted.

When the evidence disagrees

Multidomain assessment produces conflicting evidence regularly. Price may rise while breadth weakens, implied volatility increases, liquidity holds steady, and exposure concentrates. This is not automatically an analytical failure.

Evidence may conflict because the observations cover different horizons or different universes, because some of it is stale or delayed, because of measurement error, because one mechanism is expressing itself differently in different places, because the market genuinely contains opposing conditions at once, or because something is changing.

The handling is procedural. Verify the data, definitions, and provenance. Align horizons where possible. **Preserve the disagreement rather than resolving it by preference.** Reduce confidence when evidence is incomplete or stale. Do not replace missing evidence with assumptions. And state what additional observation would settle it.

Unknown, unavailable, stale, estimated, and model-dependent are all legitimate states for a piece of evidence to be in. Recording them honestly produces a weaker-sounding assessment and a stronger one.

About composite scores

The obvious next step is to combine everything into one number, and the obvious next step is where most of this discipline gets lost.

A composite can simplify communication and make change over time visible. It can also conceal domains pointing in opposite directions, unequal evidence quality, missing components, nonlinear interaction, and horizon differences.

If a composite is used, four things must survive it. Component values must remain visible, so the score can be taken apart. Timestamps and horizons must be preserved, so nothing implies false simultaneity. Missing components must be represented explicitly rather than filled in. And weights, thresholds, and version must be documented, so the construction can be inspected.

A composite should compress information without destroying traceability. A number you cannot decompose is not a summary of evidence. It is a claim wearing one.

Configurations do not last

A configuration is temporary by nature. Capacity changes. Exposure is adjusted. Variability expands and contracts. Direction strengthens, weakens, or turns. The objective is not to assign a permanent label but to observe how the arrangement evolves.

Which produces the sequence the rest of this book follows:

Current configuration → configuration change → possible state transition → possible transition pathway → visible price adjustment.

Two things about that sequence are worth flagging now, because the next two chapters are built on them. The first arrow is easy. The second is not: **not every configuration change becomes a transition**, and the difference between the two is where most confident commentary about "regime change" goes wrong.

Takeaway

The four perspectives were separated so each could be examined carefully. Separation was always temporary. Markets do not experience capacity, exposure, variability, and direction independently, and the most important information is usually in how they are arranged rather than in any of them alone. **No one perspective is enough**, and this chapter is where that stops being a caution and becomes the method.

That arrangement is a configuration, and it explains why identical returns can come from opposite mechanisms, why identical starting conditions can produce different outcomes, and why a market can be strong and fragile simultaneously without any contradiction.

Reading across domains does not produce certainty. What it produces is an assessment that states what is supported, at what confidence, from evidence of what quality, with what remaining unknown. The next chapter asks what happens when you try to compress all of that into something short enough to say out loud.

PART THREE

Market Evolution

Chapters 9–10

Most of what changes in a market is not a change in the market.

Describing a market completely takes a paragraph. Saying something about it takes a sentence. Everything lost between the two is where market communication goes wrong — a short label carries all the authority of the long description and none of its evidence.

Chapter 9 is about doing that compression deliberately, with the losses visible: what a market state is, who assigns it, what it can support, and the safeguards that keep a representation from being mistaken for the thing represented.

Chapter 10 asks the harder question. Markets move constantly. Almost none of that movement is a genuine reorganization of how a market is put together, and telling the difference is neither obvious nor free. Confirmation costs time, and the time is what buys reliability.

Both chapters end in the same place: confident about what has been observed, and considerably less confident about where it goes next. That gap is not a failure of the method. It is the method being honest.

CHAPTER NINE

Market States

You cannot say a configuration out loud

At the end of the previous chapter there was a description of a market: positive intermediate trend, narrowing breadth, concentrated leadership, contained realized volatility, rising short-dated implied volatility, normal visible spreads, slower downside replenishment, model-dependent evidence of concentrated exposure.

That is accurate and it is not usable in a sentence. You cannot compare it to last Tuesday without writing both out in full. You cannot monitor it. You cannot put it in a table with a hundred other days. And you certainly cannot say it to someone who asked how the market looks.

So people compress. They say the market is fragile, or constructive, or stretched, or fine. The compression is unavoidable and it is where most of the damage in market communication happens, because a short label carries all the authority of the long description and none of its evidence.

This chapter is about doing the compression on purpose, with the losses visible.

Who assigns the label

Start with the distinction the whole chapter rests on.

> **The market possesses a configuration. The analyst or the model assigns a state representation to selected features of that configuration.**

The market does not arrive labeled. Somebody chose which variables to include, over what horizon, normalized against what baseline, with what thresholds, sorted into what categories. A state is therefore a controlled analytical construction, not a natural object waiting to be discovered.

That has an immediate and frequently misunderstood consequence. **Two competent analysts can classify the same market differently without either making an error**, if they used different horizons, universes, purposes, or definitions. The disagreement is real and it is not necessarily about the market. It may be entirely about the two constructions. What is not acceptable is leaving the construction undocumented, so that the disagreement looks like a dispute about facts.

What a state is

> **A market state is a controlled, higher-level representation of selected features of a market configuration, for a stated purpose, horizon, universe, and method.**

Four safeguards are built into that.

It represents **selected** features. It does not contain every variable that affects the market, and the selection is a choice that can be wrong.

It applies at a **specified time and horizon**. A state without a horizon is not a claim; it is a mood.

It depends on a **defined universe and method**. Which instruments, which measurements, which thresholds.

It exists for an **analytical purpose**: description, comparison, monitoring change, research, or providing context for a decision. A state built for one purpose may be useless for another, and that is not a failure of the state.

What a state is not

	A market state is
A structured representation	The complete market
A summary of selected evidence	A single indicator
Horizon-specific	Timeless
Model- and purpose-dependent	Universally objective
Provisional	Permanent
Decomposable	A black-box score
Descriptive or diagnostic	Automatically predictive
Decision-supporting	A universal action instruction

The right-hand column is not a list of hypothetical errors. Every one of them is an ordinary reading of an ordinary market comment.

SIDEBAR

State Versus Signal

These two words get used as though one implied the other. They belong to different activities entirely.

A **state** is a representation. It answers: *how should selected features of the current configuration be summarized, for this purpose, at this horizon?* It is descriptive. It compresses evidence. It can be taken apart.

A **signal** is a rule-generated indication intended to inform a decision. It answers: *has a specified condition been met?* It is an output of a decision rule that somebody wrote, encoding somebody's objectives.

The gap between them contains everything this book has spent eight chapters establishing. To get from a state to a signal you need, at minimum: a decision the signal is meant to inform, a participant whose objectives it serves, constraints that make some responses feasible and others not, a horizon matching the decision rather than the measurement, and evidence that acting on it improves something once costs are considered.

None of that is contained in the state. A state that is descriptively valid may have no predictive value at all — and that is not a defect unless somebody claimed otherwise. Conversely, a relationship that does predict something may still be useless once transaction costs, capacity, and asymmetric consequences are taken into account.

Two neighbours are worth adding. A **regime** is a relatively persistent statistical, behavioral, or institutional environment, identified under a stated method and horizon — broader and slower than a state. A **forecast** concerns a future outcome and requires a target, a horizon, an information set, and calibration.

So: configuration is the detail. State is the summary. Regime is the environment. Signal is a rule firing. Forecast is a claim about the future. Judgment is a conclusion for a purpose. Action is what a specific participant does. Seven distinct things, routinely reported as one.

Why compress at all

The case for state representations is practical. Without them, every communication requires reprocessing dozens of measurements. With them, you can compare across time, monitor change, study history, detect transitions, construct scenarios, and implement something in software.

The cost is equally real. Detail is lost. Contradictory evidence disappears into a single word. Artificial boundaries start to look natural. Missing values get treated as though they were neutral values.

Which produces the governing rule:

A state may compress evidence, but it must not destroy traceability.

A state representation is useful only when the path back to its components remains open. If you cannot get from the label to the measurements, the label is not a summary. It is an assertion.

What gets represented

The four domains provide the primary structure — liquidity, positioning, volatility, and trend. Several cross-domain dimensions may be added when they are defined and supported: breadth and leadership, resilience, fragility or stress sensitivity, data quality, and confidence.

These dimensions are not independent of one another. Fragility, for instance, might be inferred partly from concentration, leverage, liquidity, and nonlinear exposure — all of which appear elsewhere in the same representation. A design that does not identify its own dependencies will double-count.

The Institute's formal version of this is called the **Structural State Vector**: a decomposable representation containing selected domain and cross-domain variables at a defined time and horizon. In one illustrative form it holds nine components — liquidity, positioning, volatility, trend, breadth and leadership, resilience, fragility, data quality, and confidence.

Two of those nine deserve attention, because their presence is the point. **Data quality and confidence are components of the representation, not commentary attached to it.** A state that cannot tell you how fresh and how trustworthy its own inputs were is not a governed representation.

The vector does not imply that every component is directly observable, independent, equally weighted, sufficient, or predictive. Some components are measured, some derived, some inferred from several proxies. And the governing statement is unambiguous:

> **The Structural State Vector is a governed representation of selected evidence. It is not a self-validating description of the entire market.**

A related construct, the **Market Compass**, is a visual layer for communicating selected state components — orientation, balance, divergence, confidence, and change. A responsible version shows component values, shows confidence and freshness, distinguishes established condition from recent movement, exposes mixed and unavailable components, and permits decomposition back to source measurements.

What it must never do is reduce multidomain information to a single bullish or bearish arrow. **The Compass communicates selected state components. It is not the market state, and it does not replace the measurements underneath it.** A visualization may summarize a model; it must not silently redefine one.

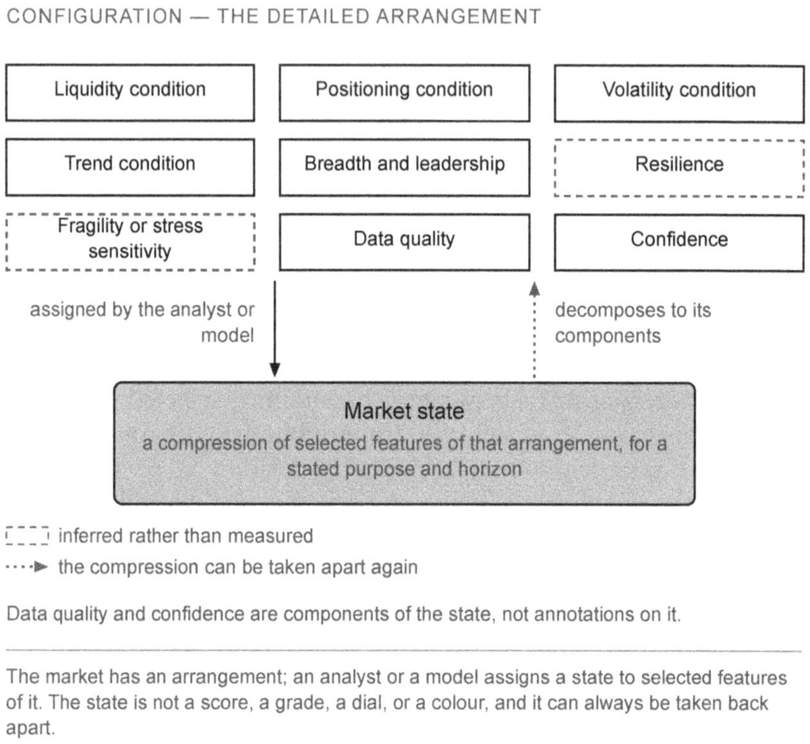

Figure 10. An arrangement compressed into a state, and taken back apart. The state is assigned, not discovered.

Categories and the boundaries they invent

Continuous values preserve magnitude and gradual change. Categories communicate faster and create discrete boundaries where the underlying quantity has none.

A liquidity-resilience percentile distinguishes modest deterioration from severe. The category "impaired" communicates more quickly and erases that distinction — along with the fact that a value just above the cutoff may be nearly identical to one just below.

The discipline: retain the continuous value where possible, display the category as a summary, and preserve the threshold that produced it.

Thresholds themselves need documentation: the rationale, the calibration period, the units, sensitivity near the boundary, the persistence rule, what happens when data are missing, and the version. **A threshold is not a natural law merely because software applies it consistently.**

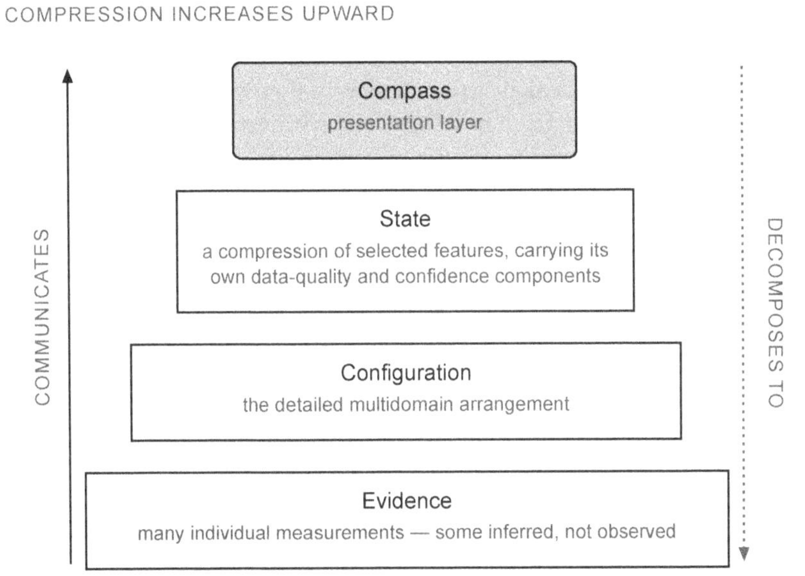

Each band compresses the one beneath it. A narrower band carries fewer components — it is not more important, not more certain, and not a conclusion.

The Compass communicates selected state components. It is not the market state itself and does not replace its measurements. There is no reading to take from it here.

Figure 11. Where the Market Compass sits. It communicates selected state components; it is not the market state itself.

Consistency is a property of the implementation. It says nothing about whether the boundary corresponds to anything in the market.

There is a related design problem. Without stabilizing rules, a classification sitting near a boundary will oscillate — flipping back and forth on noise. **Hysteresis** addresses this by requiring different evidence to enter a state than to leave it, or by requiring a minimum duration, or by imposing a confidence floor.

That improves stability and introduces lag. Too much stabilization conceals genuine rapid change; too little produces noise. There is no setting that avoids both, and a design that does not state which way it errs has hidden a decision rather than solved a problem.

Established condition and recent movement

One distinction does more practical work than any other in this chapter.

A **confirmed structural state** is the primary representation, produced over a designated evaluation horizon after requirements for evidence quality, freshness, and persistence have been satisfied.

A **fast trajectory observation** describes recent movement relative to that confirmed state, sampled over shorter intervals. It may show rotation developing well before the structural classification changes.

Both are valuable, for opposite reasons. Fast observation improves responsiveness. It is also more sensitive to noise, to event effects, and to temporary imbalance. Confirmed state improves reliability at the cost of lag.

Confirmed structural state	Fast trajectory
Primary structural representation	Recent path of multidomain change
Higher persistence requirement	Greater responsiveness
Lower sensitivity to temporary noise	Higher sensitivity to temporary noise
Used for structural description	Used for emerging rotation and monitoring
Not a forecast	Not a forecast, and not confirmation

Both should be shown together and labeled distinctly, so that responsiveness does not erase structural context and structural stability does not conceal emerging change.

One point about the horizons involved. In one implementation of this framework, five- and ten-minute observations describe fast trajectory while a thirty-minute evaluation horizon governs the confirmed structural phase. **Those numbers are implementation parameters, not market laws.** They were chosen for a particular purpose on particular instruments. Another instrument, another purpose, or another research design may require entirely different horizons, and nothing in the framework privileges any specific value.

Four related terms complete the vocabulary. **State** describes where the representation currently stands. **Trajectory** describes the direction of recent component change. **Velocity** describes how quickly components are changing. **Acceleration** describes whether that rate is increasing or decreasing.

Each requires an explicit measurement definition. "Liquidity is deteriorating rapidly" is incomplete until it names the liquidity measurement, the interval, the baseline, and the units. And a stable state can coexist with an adverse trajectory, when recent movement has not yet met the requirements for reclassification. That combination is common and is not a contradiction.

When the evidence points both ways

Markets routinely contain strength and sensitivity at once. A positive trend with narrow breadth. Low realized volatility with rising short-dated implied volatility. Normal visible spreads with weakening depth.

The temptation is to average these into "neutral." That is wrong, and specifically wrong: neutral implies balance, while the actual configuration contains opposing and material conditions. More accurate labels exist.

- **Coherent** — most components support a similar reading.
- **Mixed** — meaningful supportive and adverse conditions coexist.
- **Divergent** — domains or horizons point in different directions.
- **Transitional** — evidence indicates material change, classification unsettled.
- **Indeterminate** — available evidence does not support a reliable state.
- **Low-confidence** — a state is assigned, but support is limited.

Opposing evidence may be structurally informative. Do not erase it to produce a cleaner label. A state summary should preserve the contradiction and say which dimensions support each side.

Components that are missing, stale, or inferred

Every component should carry a quality status: current, delayed, stale, unavailable, incomplete, estimated, proxy-based, model-dependent, contradicted, invalid, or unknown.

Two rules follow, and they are the same two from Chapter 2 arriving where they do the most damage if ignored.

A missing component is not neutral. Filling a gap with a mid-range value produces a representation that looks complete and is not.

A stale component is not current. Reusing a last-known value without disclosure can make an apparently complete state materially misleading — and the staler the input, the more confident the picture will look, because nothing in it is moving.

Estimated and model-dependent values must stay distinguishable from directly observed or deterministically calculated ones. A representation that renders all of its components in the same visual weight has asserted an equivalence that does not exist.

The same market at different scales

A market may simultaneously be experiencing intraday stress, intermediate structural balance, and a positive long-horizon trend. These are not contradictory if they refer to different horizons.

Every state should identify its observation horizon, sampling interval, effective time, update cadence, universe, and model version. **"The market is stressed" is incomplete without a scale**, and most disagreements about market condition dissolve the moment both parties state theirs.

Nested states support richer reasoning and should not be collapsed into one category. Short-horizon stress may stay local. It may also be early evidence of something broader. Which of those it turns out to be is not knowable at the time, and pretending otherwise is the subject of the next chapter.

What a state is for

The reason to construct one at all is **state dependence**: the response to new information depends on the configuration receiving it.

A modest earnings disappointment may produce limited movement in a liquid, lightly positioned market and a large decline in a crowded, thin one. A state representation summarizes the receiving configuration, which supports conditional reasoning — if this arrives, the market that receives it looks like this.

What it does not do is guarantee the response, identify every relevant variable, or establish causation. **A state describes the conditions under which an event occurs. It does not determine the event's outcome.**

Duration is not stability

States can be momentary, emerging, persistent, mature, deteriorating, or transitioning. Duration can increase confidence in the description.

It does not increase confidence in the outcome. **A long-lasting state is not necessarily stable or resilient. Fragile configurations can persist for extended periods** — which is exactly why identifying fragility is not the same as identifying timing, and why the observation that "this has been going on for a while" cuts in both directions.

There is a further trap. A state model can lose relevance even when its code has not changed. Market structure changes, participant behavior changes, regulation changes, data sources change, volatility distributions change, and strategies become crowded. All of these alter what the components and thresholds mean.

A stable calculation does not guarantee a stable meaning.

A model that has not been revised in three years may be reporting faithfully on a market that no longer exists.

The danger of one number

Everything in this chapter argues against a single composite state label, and yet one is always what gets requested.

A single label can conceal opposing domains, unequal confidence, missing measurements, threshold sensitivity, model disagreement, horizon mismatch, and concentration. **Composite states are most dangerous when their simplicity is mistaken for completeness.**

The requirement is therefore firm: a state representation may compress evidence, but it must remain decomposable into component measurements, assumptions, quality states, and confidence. Every composite should preserve component values, quality states, timestamps, weights, thresholds, and version. Missing values should never be silently replaced with neutral ones.

A worked case

Consider a market with a positive intermediate trend, narrowing breadth, concentrated leadership, contained realized volatility, rising short-dated implied volatility, normal visible spreads, slower downside replenishment, and model-dependent evidence of concentrated positioning.

A defensible representation would classify trend as positive; liquidity as functional but asymmetric; positioning as concentrated, with moderate confidence; volatility as contained in realized terms but elevated in short-horizon implied terms; breadth as weak; resilience as moderate; fragility as elevated; data quality as mixed; and overall confidence in the configuration as moderate.

The confirmed structural summary might read:

> The market remains directionally positive but increasingly concentrated and adjustment-sensitive. Liquidity is functional under observed conditions, while weaker downside replenishment and narrow participation reduce structural balance. Positioning-based fragility remains model-dependent.

And the fast trajectory observation might add:

> Recent trajectory shows further breadth deterioration and short-horizon volatility expansion, but the persistence requirements for a confirmed structural change have not been satisfied.

Read those two together. The first says where things stand. The second says which way they are moving and explicitly declines to promote that movement into a change of classification. Neither says what will happen. Neither says what to do.

The line that does not get crossed

The same state can support entirely different actions for different participants. A market maker may alter inventory and quoting. A long-term investor may do nothing at all. A risk manager may reduce leverage. A tactical trader may wait for confirmation.

The differences arise from objective, horizon, mandate, capital, risk tolerance, execution constraints, and existing exposure. **The state supplies context. It does not determine a universal response**, and the fact that this needs saying is the reason Chapter 11 exists.

Common misuses

	The misuse
Treating the state as the market	The representation is selective by construction
Treating a state as a forecast	Description is not prediction
Treating trajectory as confirmed state	Fast movement may not persist
Treating missing components as neutral	Absence is not balance
Treating a composite score as an explanation	Components and mechanisms are concealed
Treating thresholds as natural boundaries	They were designed by someone
Ignoring horizon	States legitimately differ by scale
Treating a state as action guidance	Decisions depend on participant context
Preserving an outdated state	Configuration and data may have moved

Takeaway

Compression is necessary and lossy. A market state is what you get when a configuration is deliberately compressed for a stated purpose, over a stated horizon, by a stated method — and its usefulness depends entirely on whether the losses stay visible.

It is not the market, not a signal, not a forecast, and not an instruction. It is assigned rather than discovered, which means two people can disagree about it without either being wrong. It carries its own data quality and confidence as components rather than as footnotes. And it must always be possible to take it apart.

A state describes where things stand. The far more difficult question is when things have actually changed — as opposed to merely moved.

CHAPTER TEN

When Markets Change

"Everything changed today"

It is said after most bad days and some good ones. Sometimes it is right. Usually it is a description of how the day felt, applied to a market that will look substantially the same in a week.

Markets change continuously. Most of that change is minor, local, and temporary. Some of it is a genuine reorganization of how the market is put together. The analytical problem is not noticing that something moved. It is determining whether the movement was noise, ordinary variation, a local disturbance, an emerging change, a confirmed one, a change that started and failed, a stabilization, a reversal, or a structural reorganization.

Those are ten different things and they get called the same thing.

The rule that does most of the work

Start here, because everything else in the chapter follows from it.

> **All confirmed state transitions involve configuration change, but most configuration changes do not become confirmed transitions.**

Configurations change constantly. Depth thins and rebuilds. Breadth wobbles. Implied volatility rises before an event and falls after it. Exposure shifts as positions roll. Almost none of this constitutes a transition in the sense that matters, and the ability to tell the difference is most of what this chapter offers.

A **market transition** is a material reorganization of selected configuration features through time, evaluated against a stated baseline, horizon, and classification method. A **state transition** is the classification event that occurs when that reorganization satisfies defined requirements for materiality, persistence, evidence quality, and thresholds.

Those two are related and not identical, and the distinction is worth holding. The market process is something that happens. The classification event is something a method does about it. A market can reorganize substantially without any method having yet confirmed it, and a method can confirm a change that subsequently unwinds.

What a transition is not

	A transition may be
A material configuration change	Every price move
A multidomain reorganization	A universal regime shift
An emerging process	A guaranteed destination
A method-defined classification change	A natural boundary visible to everyone
A provisional conclusion	A permanent label
A monitored pathway	A forecast
A reversible development	Irreversible
Decision-relevant context	A universal instruction

Five related terms are worth separating, because they are used as though they were a single escalating scale and they are not.

Term	What it means
Change	Any measurable difference through time
Disturbance	A short-lived or localized disruption
Transition	A material reorganization toward a different state representation
Regime shift	A relatively persistent change in the broader environment or governing relationships
Structural break	A change that weakens the validity of prior process assumptions

Every regime shift includes transition. Not every transition becomes a regime shift. A one-session volatility event is a disturbance. A multi-month change in inflation, policy, and correlation structure may be a regime shift. Calling the first the second is the most common overstatement in market commentary, and it costs nothing to make, which is why it is made so often.

What counts as evidence

A price decline establishes direction and magnitude. It does not establish impaired capacity, forced selling, structural deterioration, or a new state.

Stronger transition evidence combines observations that are relevant, timely, and sufficiently independent of one another: material changes in components, persistence across the defined horizon, breadth across instruments or domains, coherent interaction between domains rather than one domain moving alone, movement across thresholds, changes in resilience and feedback, and evidence quality sufficient to support a classification at all.

That evidence gets evaluated along several dimensions, because no single one is adequate. **Magnitude** — how large. **Persistence** — how long it has held. **Breadth** — how widely distributed. **Coherence** — whether domains support a common reading. **Speed** — how rapidly the configuration is moving. **Reversibility** — how easily it could return. Plus how structurally significant the change is, whether its rate is increasing, and how much confidence the evidence supports.

Where a change is in its development

The most useful practical vocabulary in this chapter is a set of labels for how far a change has gotten. They describe **evidentiary development**, not certainty about where it ends.

Label	What it means
Isolated	A brief or local change with limited support
Emerging	Several observations begin to support material change
Developing	Magnitude, breadth, or persistence is increasing
Confirmed	Governed transition requirements are satisfied
Mature	The new configuration has persisted and broadened
Stabilizing	The rate of change is slowing
Reversing	Evidence supports movement back, or toward another state
Failed	The change does not persist under the method

Notice the last one. A change can reach "confirmed" and then fail. This is not a flaw in the labeling; it is an accurate description of markets, in which things genuinely start and then genuinely stop.

Responsiveness against reliability

Every transition method faces the same unavoidable trade-off, and no design escapes it.

Early indication emphasizes responsiveness: recent evidence suggesting possible change. **Confirmation** emphasizes reliability: the designated requirements for materiality, persistence, and evidence quality having been met.

A system that reacts quickly will classify ordinary variation as structural change. A system that waits will describe a transition only after it has become obvious to everyone, at which point the description is accurate and no longer useful.

Confirmation requires evidence, and evidence requires time. Sampling intervals, lookback windows, persistence rules, data delays, missing values, stabilization rules, and recalculation all create lag.

Lag is the cost of requiring evidence. It is not always a defect — it is frequently what prevents false alarms. But excessive lag can make a representation operationally irrelevant, and there is no setting at which both problems disappear. What a responsible design does is state which way it errs and why, and validate that choice against the purpose it serves.

SIDEBAR

Fast Change Versus Confirmed Transition

On a day when a market moves sharply, two entirely different statements are available, and they are constantly confused.

"The configuration is moving quickly." This is an observation about recent trajectory. Depth is thinning faster than usual. Breadth is deteriorating within the session. Short-dated implied volatility is expanding. All of it can be true, measured, and important — and none of it is a change in classification.

"The structural state has changed." This is a classification event. It requires that the change be material, that it persist across a defined horizon, that the underlying evidence meet quality requirements, and that whatever thresholds the method specifies have been crossed and held.

The distance between these is where most premature conclusions live. Fast movement is what you notice. Confirmation is what you can defend.

Both belong on the same screen, labeled separately. Showing only the trajectory produces a market that appears to be in constant upheaval. Showing only the confirmed state produces one that appears calm right up until it does not.

Two cautions. Speed of change is not evidence of significance: a rapidly moving noisy measure can look more important than a slower but structurally meaningful shift. And whether the rate of change is itself increasing — acceleration — is a second-order estimate, considerably more sensitive to noise, sampling, and smoothing than the level it is derived from, and it requires stronger caution rather than less.

Changes that start and stop

A **false transition** occurs when evidence briefly approaches or meets the criteria and the configuration then returns toward the prior state. Causes include temporary event risk, spikes in thin conditions, data errors, expiration effects, participants closing positions under pressure, oscillation near a boundary, and model sensitivity.

False transitions should be recorded rather than quietly discarded, because they reveal exactly where a method sits on the responsiveness–reliability trade-off.

And crucially: **not every failed transition is a model error.** Some genuine changes begin and then reverse, because participants adapt, because balancing forces became dominant, or because the pathway simply changed. A failed transition may represent a real but non-persistent change. Treating every failure as a mistake in the method leads to overtuning a system against markets that were behaving normally.

Stabilizing rules help. Requiring different evidence to enter a state than to leave it, imposing a minimum duration before reclassification, or requiring a confidence floor all reduce unstable switching. Each of them also delays detection. The rules should be transparent and should be tested against genuine rapid change as well as against noise, because a design tuned only against noise will be reliably late when something real happens.

The trigger explains the timing

When a market reorganizes, attention goes to whatever happened immediately beforehand: an earnings announcement, a policy decision, an economic release, a margin event, a geopolitical shock.

The trigger is worth identifying and it explains less than it appears to.

> **The trigger helps explain when change began. The receiving configuration helps explain how it propagated and how large it became.**

The full structure is worth having in mind. A **trigger** is the event associated with initiation. A **proximate mechanism** is the immediate transmission process: sell orders consuming available bids. A **structural condition** is the configuration that determines sensitivity: concentrated exposure, thin capacity. A **feedback mechanism** reinforces or limits the adjustment. And the **outcome** is what is observed.

Explanations that stop at the trigger are the ones that age worst, because the same trigger arriving a month earlier or later would have produced a different outcome, and nothing about the trigger explains why.

Some configurations are more sensitive to disturbance than others: concentrated or leveraged exposure, thin or asymmetric capacity, narrow leadership, unstable volatility structure, weak replenishment, funding or collateral sensitivity, and crowded strategy use.

These are contributory and conditional. **They do not guarantee transition, establish direction, or identify timing.** A fragile configuration may persist until a trigger arrives, or may repair itself without any notable event. This is the same limitation Chapter 9 raised about duration, arriving in the place where it is most tempting to forget it.

Pathways that amplify, and pathways that stop

A **reinforcing pathway** amplifies change. A downside version might run: adverse price movement, then risk reduction, then consumption of available capacity, then greater price impact, then volatility expansion, then tighter limits, then additional selling, then trend deterioration, then further repositioning.

That sequence is a representation of interaction, not an object anyone observes. The actual order may differ. Several steps may occur at once. And the loop can be interrupted at any point.

Because **balancing pathways** oppose change and support stabilization: value-based demand entering, those supplying liquidity returning, forced selling completing, policy response, hedging demand being satisfied, volatility normalizing, portfolio rebalancing, and depth recovering.

Presenting the first list without the second is not simplification. It describes a market with no mechanism for stopping, which is not the market anyone actually trades in. Most reinforcing sequences terminate, and they terminate for reasons.

One important note about how they terminate: **a transition may stabilize in a new state without reversing to the prior one.** Stabilization does not mean things went back. The market may settle into a different configuration after substantial reorganization, and frequently does.

Partial, failed, reversed, stabilized, recovered

Five outcomes get confused, and separating them is straightforward once named.

An **incomplete transition** occurs when some components change materially and others do not. Volatility expands while trend holds. Breadth deteriorates while capacity stays resilient. Exposure concentrates without visible stress. The honest labels are partial, uneven, domain-specific, unresolved, or stalled — rather than forcing a complete classification. The unaligned components may later confirm, repair, or stay divergent indefinitely.

A **failed transition** is one that does not persist and moves back toward the prior state. Discussed above. Valuable as evidence about which signposts distinguish persistence from reversal.

A **reversal** is not simply a move against the prevailing direction. A confirmed reversal may require sustained opposing movement, breadth confirmation, a change in leadership, altered volatility and liquidity structure, changed positioning, and persistence beyond a temporary disturbance. **Countertrend movement is not automatically a state reversal**, and an intraday reversal can occur entirely within an unchanged intermediate trend.

Stabilization means the rate of adverse change slows or stops. Spreads cease widening. Depth begins replenishing. Volatility stops accelerating. Breadth stops deteriorating. Forced activity declines.

Recovery means selected conditions have actually improved: liquidity restoration, volatility normalization, broader participation, better trend structure, reduced concentration, higher confidence.

The two are routinely reported as one event and they are not. **Stabilization means deterioration has slowed. Recovery means conditions have improved.** A market can stabilize at an impaired level and stay there. Whether it recovers, stalls in a range, or resumes deteriorating is an empirical question, and nothing about stabilization answers it.

WHAT HAPPENS TO A CONFIRMED TRANSITION

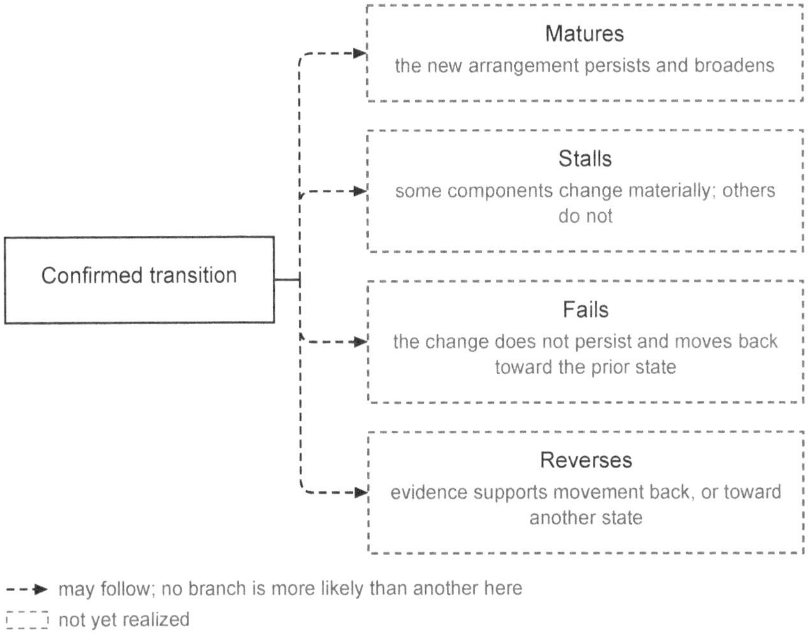

A confirmed transition may mature, stall, fail, or reverse. It may also stabilize, which the text treats separately. Confidence that a transition is under way is not confidence in where it ends, and no branch here carries a probability.

Figure 12. What can happen to a confirmed transition. Confidence that a transition is under way is not confidence in where it ends.

Transitions have scales

An intraday transition into stress can occur while the intermediate structural state and the long-horizon environment remain entirely unchanged.

Every transition claim should identify its observation horizon, confirmation horizon, effective time, update cadence, universe, and model version. **A transition at one horizon does not automatically imply a transition at another.**

Nested horizons provide early context and also create apparent contradiction. The contradiction should be preserved and explained rather than resolved by choosing whichever horizon supports the preferred conclusion.

Where a transition starts

Transitions begin in different places, and the starting point is informative without being the whole explanation.

Lead	Illustrative first evidence
Liquidity-led	Depth loss, spread widening, impact increasing
Positioning-led	Forced adjustment, concentration, hedging demand
Volatility-led	Rapid change in realized or implied variability
Trend-led	Breadth and directional structure deteriorating
Information-led	Repricing after new information

The initiating domain should not be treated automatically as the sole cause. The other domains determine how far it propagates and whether it stabilizes.

Transitions may also spread across markets — through collateral and margin, common ownership and balance sheets, derivative hedging, portfolio rebalancing, leverage reduction, index and basis relationships, and strategies targeting a level of variability. Observing that several markets moved together does not identify which channel carried it. Timing, institutional relationships, common exposures, and alternative explanations all have to be evaluated before a channel can be claimed.

Confident that it is changing, uncertain where it goes

This is the distinction that separates disciplined transition analysis from forecasting dressed as analysis.

Confidence in a transition should stay separate from confidence in the current state, in the destination, in the cause, and in any prediction. The evidence may strongly support that a configuration is changing while leaving the destination genuinely open.

A well-formed assessment sounds like this: *high confidence that the configuration is changing; moderate confidence that a confirmed transition is underway; low confidence regarding the destination; and low predictive confidence regarding the price outcome.*

Those are four separate statements and collapsing them loses the information that made the assessment worth making.

Confidence that a transition is underway does not imply confidence in its destination.

A deteriorating positive state may return to the prior state, settle into balance, become stressed, reverse direction, or stabilize in a configuration nobody had a name for. Destination uncertainty should not be concealed by naming the transition after its most feared or most desired outcome.

Which yields one of the most practically useful sentences in this book: **"emerging deterioration" is more defensible than "bear market beginning"** when the destination is unresolved. The first is a claim about evidence. The second is a claim about the future wearing the clothes of a claim about evidence.

A transition that confirms

Initial configuration. Intermediate trend positive, breadth moderate, volatility low, liquidity functional, positioning increasingly concentrated. The confirmed structural state is directionally positive.

Emerging evidence. Breadth narrows. Downside depth replenishes more slowly. Short-dated implied volatility rises. Leadership concentration increases. Fast trajectory deteriorates.

The appropriate reading at this stage: the market remains in a positive confirmed state and is becoming more concentrated and less resilient. Not a transition. A trajectory, and a change in the character of the configuration.

Later evidence. Breadth deteriorates further. Spreads widen. Price impact rises. Trend structure weakens. Positioning estimates indicate greater downside sensitivity. The persistence criteria are met.

The governed state then transitions toward a fragile, adjustment-sensitive condition.

And now the sentence that the entire example exists to support: **the confirmed transition does not establish that a major decline must follow.** What it establishes is that the selected configuration features have reorganized under the method. What happens next depends on what arrives, what participants do, and how the new configuration receives it.

Stress that is not a transition

The counterweight case is just as important, and it is the one that gets omitted from most treatments.

Consider a sharp intraday decline accompanied by realized-volatility expansion, higher implied volatility, and surging volume. It looks severe. The commentary will say so.

But spreads remain proportionate to the movement. Depth replenishes after being consumed. Broad forced selling does not emerge. The intermediate trend stays intact. Conditions normalize by the close.

The disciplined assessment: the market experienced a short-horizon disturbance and temporary stress. The evidence did not satisfy the requirements for a confirmed structural transition.

That is a genuinely useful conclusion, and it is unpublishable, because it consists of saying that a dramatic day was a dramatic day. Which is precisely why the discipline matters. **The number of days that feel like a transition substantially exceeds the number that are one**, and a method that cannot say so is not a method.

Common misuses

	The misuse
Treating every move as a transition	Most variation is not structural
Treating early indication as confirmation	Evidence may not persist
Treating confirmation as prediction	State change does not determine the future path
Treating the destination as known	Transitions branch, stall, and fail
Ignoring horizon	Different scales legitimately disagree
Ignoring false transitions	Reliability becomes overstated
Treating a threshold crossing as a natural boundary	Thresholds were designed
Confusing stabilization with recovery	Change can stop without improving
Confusing countertrend movement with reversal	Persistence and structure matter

Takeaway

Markets change constantly, and almost none of it is a transition. The difference is not the size of the move; it is whether selected features of the configuration have reorganized materially and persistently under a stated method.

The trigger explains when something started. The configuration explains how far it went. Fast movement is trajectory, not confirmation. Confirmation costs time, and the time is what buys reliability. Reinforcing pathways have balancing counterparts, and most sequences terminate.

And the destination stays open longer than anyone finds comfortable. Being confident that a market is changing is a different thing from knowing what it is changing into, and the discipline of saying so is what separates an assessment from a forecast.

Which leaves the question this book has deferred since Chapter 1. If you now have a defensible view of what a market looks like and how it is changing — what should you do about it? The answer turns out to depend almost entirely on who you are.

PART FOUR

Market Judgment

Chapter 11 and the Conclusion

The evidence is common. The decision is not.

Everything to this point has been about markets. This part is about people, because no amount of analysis determines what anyone should do.

Two participants can agree completely about what a market looks like and act in opposite directions without either being irrational. Their objectives differ, their obligations differ, their horizons differ, and their capacity to absorb a loss differs. Those are properties of the participant, not of the market, and no market assessment contains them.

Chapter 11 is about what a good decision under uncertainty actually looks like, and about the uncomfortable fact that its quality cannot be judged by its outcome.

The conclusion returns to the question this book has been answering all along: how do you tell whether a claim about markets deserves your trust? It is also where the framework states, at length, what it does not establish — which is the condition under which anything else in the book can be believed.

CHAPTER ELEVEN

Deciding Under Uncertainty

Three people, one market

Suppose the assessment is finished, and it reads roughly like this.

A capitalization-weighted index continues to advance while breadth narrows and leadership concentrates. Short-dated implied volatility is rising. Liquidity remains functional but is increasingly asymmetric, absorbing buying more readily than selling. Positioning estimates suggest possible adjustment sensitivity, though those estimates are model-dependent. Descriptive confidence is moderate. Predictive confidence is low.

Now consider three participants looking at that same paragraph.

A long-term unleveraged investor may maintain exposure, rebalance the concentration that has built up in the largest holdings, and monitor for evidence of transition. Their horizon is long. Their capacity to absorb a decline is relatively high. Nothing in the assessment threatens anything essential.

A leveraged short-horizon trader may reduce size, tighten limits, or wait for broader confirmation. Their margin and drawdown constraints are tighter. The same sentence about asymmetric liquidity means something operationally different to someone who may need to exit quickly.

A market-neutral options portfolio may adjust hedging frequency or reduce short convexity. Their relevant exposure is not index direction at all. It is variability and nonlinear risk, and the assessment's most important sentence for them is the one about implied volatility.

The market assessment is identical. Three rational responses, all different.

This is not a failure of the analysis. It is the point at which analysis stops and something else begins.

	FAVORABLE OUTCOME	UNFAVORABLE OUTCOME
Sound process	Good process, favorable realization	Good process, adverse realization
Poor process	Poor process, favorable luck	Poor process, adverse realization

One favorable or unfavorable outcome is insufficient to establish decision quality. All four cells are drawn identically: the figure marks none of them as the good case.

Figure 13. Process against outcome. One favorable or unfavorable outcome is insufficient to establish decision quality.

What is being evaluated

Decision quality is the degree to which a choice is made through a coherent, evidence-informed, objective-aligned, constraint-aware, uncertainty-conscious, and reviewable process. It concerns how the decision was *formed*, not whether the result was favorable.

A high-quality process generally defines the question, identifies who is responsible, states objectives, records constraints, compares realistic alternatives, uses relevant evidence, expresses uncertainty honestly, calibrates how much to commit, plans implementation, specifies what to monitor, and preserves a record of the reasoning as it existed at the time.

It does not require perfect information. In markets, delay is costly and information is incomplete by design. The standard is not omniscience. It is whether the process was proportionate to the stakes, used the best reasonably available evidence, and stayed open to revision.

SIDEBAR

A Good Decision Can Lose Money

Financial decisions are made before the future is known and evaluated after an outcome is visible. That asymmetry produces two of the most persistent errors in the field.

Hindsight bias: once an outcome is known, the warning signs seem more obvious than they were, ambiguous evidence gets reinterpreted, and alternatives that seemed plausible get forgotten.

Outcome bias: the quality of a decision gets judged by its result.

The four combinations are worth writing out, because only two of them are ever discussed.

Process	Outcome	What it actually was
Sound	Favorable	Good process, favorable realization
Sound	Unfavorable	Good process, adverse realization
Poor	Favorable	Poor process, favorable luck
Poor	Unfavorable	Poor process, adverse realization

The two middle rows are where all the learning is, and both are routinely misread. A disciplined risk reduction followed by a rally looks foolish. An oversized position on a rumor that happened to work looks like insight.

One favorable or unfavorable outcome is insufficient to establish decision quality. A single result is evidence, and rarely enough of it. Repeated poor outcomes may reveal faulty assumptions, poor calibration, model drift, weak execution, or unrealistic objectives. Repeated favorable outcomes may reflect skill, luck, hidden risk, or all three.

The practical consequence is uncomfortable: you cannot evaluate your decisions by looking at your results, at least not one at a time. You have to evaluate the process separately and then examine the two together across many decisions.

Six layers, not one

	Layer
Assessment	What does the evidence support?
Judgment	What conclusions are defensible for this purpose?
Decision	Which alternative should be selected?
Action	How will the choice be implemented?
Outcome	What happened?
Review	What should be learned or revised?

These overlap in practice, and separating them improves accountability. A participant may agree entirely with an assessment and act differently because their constraints differ. A sound decision may be implemented badly. Excellent execution may carry out a weak decision. A favorable outcome may follow from any of these.

The Decision Environment

Everything that turns an assessment into a choice sits in one structure.

A Decision Environment is the structured combination of objectives, constraints, alternatives, information, uncertainty, horizon, risk capacity, implementation conditions, and responsibility relevant to a particular choice.

It exists to stop market analysis being converted directly into generic instructions. The relevant question is not whether a market looks favorable or unfavorable. It is whether a particular action fits a particular participant in a particular environment.

The same market evidence may support different rational actions in different Decision Environments.

The components are worth walking through, because most of them get skipped.

Objectives. A decision cannot be evaluated without knowing what it is meant to achieve: maximizing expected return, preserving capital, meeting liabilities, tracking a benchmark, maintaining liquidity, reducing variability, hedging a known exposure, generating income, or satisfying a legal duty. These conflict routinely. Greater return may require lower liquidity. Faster action may reduce evidence quality. Protection costs money continuously. Responsible design makes the conflicts explicit rather than hiding them inside a single score. A decision is not good in the abstract; it is good or poor relative to stated objectives.

Constraints. These determine which alternatives are actually available: capital, leverage, liquidity, mandate, regulation, taxes, time, concentration limits, operational capacity, execution access, knowledge, funding, collateral, authority, and psychological tolerance. A theoretically attractive action may be unavailable in practice. A strategy that depends on continuous liquidity is unsuitable for someone who might have to exit quickly. **An unavailable alternative is not a genuine option.** And a preference can be traded off, while a hard legal, fiduciary, funding, or survival constraint cannot.

Alternatives. A decision process should compare realistic options rather than a preferred action against an undefined opposite. And the status quo is one of them. **Maintaining an existing position, holding cash, or postponing a change all have consequences and opportunity costs.** Treating the status quo as neutral hides those consequences and biases everything toward inertia. Note also that deliberate deferral and passive non-decision look identical from outside and are completely different: the first states why waiting is valuable, what information is expected, and when the question will be revisited.

Horizon. The decision horizon is distinct from the measurement horizon, the market-state horizon, the forecast horizon, the holding period, the review interval, and the liability horizon. These frequently differ, and horizon mismatch is one of the most common sources of error. A valid short-horizon observation can be entirely irrelevant to a long-horizon decision, and a long-horizon thesis can be inadequate for a short-horizon risk control.

Information available at the time. A decision record should preserve what was known, estimated, assumed, unavailable, stale, and uncertain when the decision was made. This is the only defense against hindsight reconstruction, and it also distinguishes information that was available but ignored — a process failure — from information that genuinely did not exist, which is ordinary uncertainty.

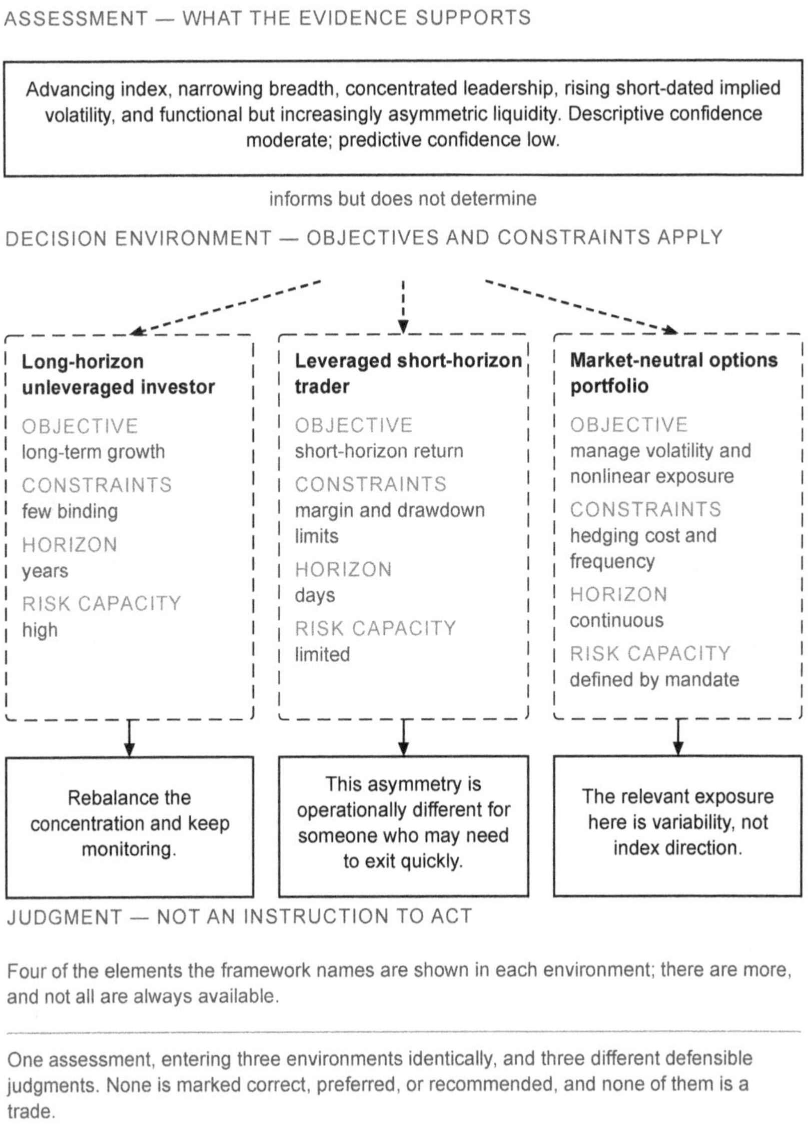

Figure 14. One assessment, entering three Decision Environments identically, and three different defensible judgments.

Uncertainty is not one thing

Data may be incomplete. Measurements may be noisy. Models may disagree. The current state may be uncertain. A transition may be real with an unclear destination. The mechanism may be contested. Execution may differ from expectation. Conditions may change after acting.

Collapsing these into a single confidence score destroys useful distinctions. A participant may hold high confidence in the current state, moderate confidence that a transition is underway, low confidence in its destination, and high confidence that existing exposure exceeds their capacity to absorb loss. That combination can justify decisive action, and it could not be represented at all by one number.

Two related cautions. **Confidence is not probability**: a model may output 60% while confidence in the model itself is low. And **a numerical probability is not automatically more rigorous than a qualitative judgment.** A meaningful probability requires a defined event, a horizon, a reference class, a model, data, and calibration. Without those, a number is decoration. Qualitative judgments can be rigorous when their definitions, evidence, and track record are clear.

Weighing outcomes

Comparing actions by weighting possible outcomes against their likelihood is a useful discipline. It is also not a complete definition of rationality.

Its result depends entirely on the probability estimates, the values assigned to outcomes, the horizon, and the range of outcomes considered. It can ignore path dependence, liquidity, model error, correlation, survival constraints, and the difference between a decision made once and a decision made repeatedly.

Two consequences follow, and they point in opposite directions.

A favorable expected value can coexist with unacceptable risk of ruin. **A favorable expected value does not justify exposure that threatens essential obligations or survival.** Repeated favorable bets are only favorable if you are still there to repeat them.

Conversely, an action with an unfavorable expected financial value can be entirely rational. Insurance is the standard case: paying a premium with negative expected monetary value in order to protect something essential.

Both follow from the fact that two participants can assign completely different values to the same market outcome. Value depends on wealth, liabilities, drawdown limits, mandate, consumption needs, career consequences, survival, and ethical obligations. A 10% decline means something entirely different to a fully funded long-term investor, a leveraged trader near a margin threshold, and a fiduciary responsible for distributions next quarter.

Market outcomes are common observations. Their decision value is participant-dependent.

Which is why **asymmetry** often matters more than any forecast. The relevant questions are the plausible upside, the plausible downside, whether adverse outcomes are survivable, whether the action is reversible, whether any impairment would be permanent, and whether one side of the payoff is capped while the other is open-ended. A modest expected gain is unattractive if the downside threatens something essential. A low-probability protection can be valuable if it guards against something catastrophic. And asymmetry has to be evaluated across a participant's whole situation, not within the instrument being considered.

Four words that are not interchangeable

Term	What it means
Risk tolerance	Willingness to experience variability or loss
Risk capacity	Ability to absorb loss without violating essential objectives
Risk appetite	The level of risk chosen to be assumed
Risk limit	A governed boundary constraining exposure regardless of belief

These get conflated constantly, and the conflations are consequential. Someone may tolerate volatility emotionally while lacking the financial capacity to absorb it. An institution may have capacity and adopt a lower appetite because of fiduciary obligations. A trader may remain entirely confident in a thesis and still be required to reduce when a limit is reached.

Where survival or essential obligations are at stake, capacity should generally dominate preference. That is not a risk-management platitude; it is a direct consequence of the asymmetry above.

Choosing under model uncertainty

A **robust** decision performs acceptably across several plausible scenarios, rather than optimally under one fragile forecast. Robustness can involve smaller commitment, diversification, staging, hedging, preserving liquidity, using reversible structures, or reducing dependence on any single assumption.

Optimization is valuable when the model is stable and the probabilities are well estimated. Under substantial model uncertainty, an apparently optimal choice can fail sharply when one assumption turns out to be wrong. Robustness trades some efficiency in the base case for resilience across alternatives.

It also should not become an excuse for permanent indecision. It is a design principle for choosing actions that remain acceptable when the future differs from the preferred forecast.

Closely related: **reversibility**. Decisions differ in how easily they can be revised, depending on transaction costs, depth, lockups, path dependence, tax consequences, and legal commitments. A reversible decision permits learning after partial commitment. That flexibility has value when uncertainty is expected to resolve over time.

Optionality is not free. Reversible structures may cost more, return less immediately, or delay commitment. Their value has to be compared against the cost of being wrong in an irreversible one.

And **more information is not automatically better**. Additional information has value when it can change the selected action enough to justify its cost and the delay. It may arrive too late, prove unreliable, duplicate what is already known, or simply fail to affect the choice. The question to ask is: which uncertainty would this reduce, would the decision actually change, how costly is waiting, and will the opportunity still exist.

Action is not binary

	Choice
Act	Evidence and asymmetry justify commitment
Act partially	Direction is supported but uncertainty remains material
Wait	Delay preserves value without excessive opportunity cost
Investigate	Additional information could materially change the choice
Hedge	Exposure must remain but adverse consequences should be reduced
Abstain	Available alternatives do not meet minimum standards

Each of these can be correct in the appropriate Decision Environment. None of them is correct in general, and this table is a taxonomy of what is available rather than guidance about when to use each.

Commitment — size, timing, duration, leverage, irreversibility — should reflect the downside, risk capacity, liquidity, correlation with existing exposure, model uncertainty, horizon, and portfolio interaction. Notably, not confidence alone. A high-confidence judgment can still justify small commitment when adverse consequences are severe or liquidity is poor. A lower-confidence judgment can justify protection when the cost is acceptable and the exposure threatens something essential.

> **Uncertainty should affect the magnitude, timing, and reversibility of commitment — not merely the language used to describe the decision.**

Three things should be kept separate, and are almost never separated. **Confidence** describes the strength of support for an assessment. **Decision margin** — an Institute term for the degree by which the preferred alternative exceeds the next-best one under stated assumptions — describes how much better one option is than another. **Commitment** describes magnitude and irreversibility.

High confidence can coexist with a narrow margin when two alternatives are nearly equally good. Moderate confidence can coexist with a wide margin when one action protects against something severe. Low confidence can justify urgent protection when capacity is limited. Keeping these apart prevents confidence from silently becoming a sizing variable, which is its most common and least examined role.

Decision margin is offered as a transparent analytical device rather than an established universal term, and it should be treated as such.

Scenarios, and how to keep them honest

A scenario is a structured conditional pathway used to organize uncertainty. It is not a declaration that the pathway will occur.

Scenario	Market pathway	Consequence for a participant
Orderly continuation	Direction persists with stable liquidity	Opportunity remains; moderate risk
Fragile continuation	Direction persists while concentration increases	Gains possible; sensitivity elevated
Stress transition	Liquidity weakens and variability expands	Loss and execution risk rise
Repair	Breadth and resilience improve	Prior concern weakens
Indeterminate	Evidence remains mixed	Decision confidence low

Each scenario should identify its starting configuration, the pathway, the **signposts** that would indicate it is developing, the consequences for the participant's objectives, and the **invalidating conditions** that would rule it out. Probabilities should not be attached unless the method is defined and calibrated.

A scenario set has to include disconfirming possibilities. Otherwise it is a narrative built to defend a decision that was already made.

The companion technique is **sensitivity**: testing whether the preferred action changes when probabilities, costs, expected returns, loss severity, liquidity, correlation, horizon, or model assumptions change. **If a small change in an assumption reverses the decision, the decision is fragile** — which may justify gathering more information, committing less, staging, or choosing a more robust alternative.

The human parts

Biases distort evidence selection, probability judgment, action, and evaluation. Evidence biases include confirmation bias and anchoring. Probability biases include overconfidence and neglect of tail outcomes. Action biases include inertia, escalation of commitment, and the sunk-cost effect. Evaluation biases include hindsight and outcome bias. Social biases include groupthink and authority pressure.

Naming a bias is not analysis. **A bias label should not substitute for identifying which evidence was ignored, which assumption became distorted, or which alternative was excluded.**

Emotion is not simply irrationality. Fear, excitement, regret, and stress may accurately reflect stakes. They can also distort attention, horizon, risk perception, and urgency. The goal is not to eliminate emotion but to govern it: precommitment, checklists, cooling periods, independent review, limits, decision logs, escalation rules. Emotional awareness can itself be evidence — a strong urge to act may indicate that exposure, incentives, or identity have become entangled with the decision.

Incentives can compromise a technically sophisticated process entirely. Compensation, career risk, benchmark pressure, marketing incentives, client retention, performance periods, personal ownership, and sponsorship of a model all influence conclusions. Material conflicts belong in the record. A rigorous method applied by someone who benefits from one answer is not a neutral method.

Groups improve decisions by combining expertise and challenging assumptions, and degrade them through diffusion of responsibility, conformity, dominance, and compromise without coherence. Useful controls include independent initial estimates, explicit dissent, designated challenge, clear authority, and preservation of minority views. **Consensus is not evidence of quality.** It may reflect shared reasoning, or shared incentives.

Automation can organize evidence, enforce limits, monitor thresholds, calculate exposures, compare scenarios, and execute consistently. It does not eliminate model risk, objective ambiguity, unknown conditions, or responsibility. A system can optimize the wrong objective, act on stale data, or execute a badly governed rule with great consistency. **Automation changes the mechanism of action. It does not remove accountability.**

Writing it down

A decision record turns reasoning into something that can be reviewed later. It does not need to be long, and it should be proportionate to the stakes.

Field	What it captures
The question	What choice is being made
Objectives	What the action is intended to achieve
Constraints	What limits the feasible choices
Alternatives	What was actually compared, including doing nothing
Assessment and confidence	What the evidence supports, and how strongly, by claim type
Selected action and commitment	What was chosen, at what size, timing, and reversibility
Monitoring	Which signposts require attention
Revision conditions	What would change or invalidate this

The purpose is not paperwork. It is that organizations and individuals reliably remember outcomes and forget the uncertainty that existed beforehand. Without a record, every past decision looks either obvious or inexplicable.

Two review practices are worth the time. A **pre-mortem** asks participants to assume the decision has failed and identify plausible causes. It reverses the natural tendency to defend a preferred action and surfaces hidden dependencies. And **independent challenge** assigns someone to attack the evidence, assumptions, alternatives, and implementation. Both must be capable of changing the decision; otherwise they are procedure rather than review.

After the decision

A decision is not complete at implementation. Monitoring should specify expected signposts, contrary evidence, changes in state or transition, execution quality, limit usage, time-based review, and model drift.

Revising a decision when the evidence changes is disciplined adaptation, not inconsistency. A good process commits to an objective and a method, not to defending an outdated conclusion. Equally, continuous revision becomes instability; monitoring rules should distinguish ordinary variation from information that materially changes the rationale.

Four concepts should stay separate here. An **exit condition** requires terminating or reducing an action. An **invalidation condition** indicates the original rationale no longer holds. A **review condition** requires reassessment. A **risk limit** constrains exposure regardless of belief. A limit may require reduction while the thesis remains entirely valid. A review may occur without any action. An invalidation may change the thesis before an exit is practically possible. Merging them permits reinterpretation after losses, which is when reinterpretation is least trustworthy.

When something goes wrong, review the whole chain rather than the outcome: was material information missing, stale, or ignored; did the inference exceed the evidence; was the model inappropriate; was confidence systematically overstated; were alternatives and constraints poorly framed; was execution different from the plan; were limits absent or ignored; or was the outcome simply a plausible adverse realization of a sound process.

The same analysis should follow favorable outcomes. A profit can conceal ignored evidence, excessive size, poor execution, or an unrecognized tail exposure. Learning requires examining process regardless of how the result felt.

One caution about **counterfactuals**. Asking what would have happened under a different choice supports learning and remains uncertain, because the alternative outcome was not observed. A hedge looks unnecessary because the adverse event did not occur. An avoided investment later rises. A position closed at a loss recovers. None of these establishes that the original decision was poor, without considering the information and objectives that existed at the time. Counterfactuals should be treated as estimates with assumptions attached, not as facts.

Two cases

Sound process, adverse outcome. A risk manager reduces concentrated exposure because liquidity is deteriorating, variability is expanding, downside sensitivity is increasing, and the institution's capacity to absorb loss is limited. The market rebounds immediately afterward.

The rebound does not establish that the decision was wrong. The evidence was current. The assessment was reasonable. The exposure exceeded capacity. The action reduced tail risk. The review should still examine whether the reduction was larger than necessary, whether staging would have been better, whether the thresholds were well calibrated, and whether execution cost too much. But those are questions about the process, not about the rebound.

Decision quality is not immunity from loss.

Poor process, favorable outcome. A participant takes an oversized position based on an unverified claim circulating on social media, without examining liquidity, downside, conflicting evidence, or their own capacity to absorb loss. The asset rises sharply.

The favorable outcome validates none of it: not the information source, not the sizing, not the absence of risk controls, not the reasoning. And interpreting luck as skill makes the next decision more dangerous, because the participant will now have more confidence in a method that has not been tested.

The correct review separates the profit from the process and asks whether the same method would remain acceptable across many decisions and many adverse realizations.

Responsibility

Decision quality includes more than profitability. It may involve fiduciary duty, fairness, market integrity, client suitability, disclosure, conflicts, the use of confidential information, and consequences for people other than the decision maker.

A decision can be profitable and still be irresponsible. An action that exploits a client's information disadvantage, violates a mandate, conceals conflicts, or transfers unacceptable risk to someone else does not become high-quality because it made money.

Responsibility begins earlier than most people place it: in how objectives are defined, whose interests they represent, which consequences are considered, and who bears the downside.

Takeaway

No market assessment determines what anyone should do. The evidence is common; the decision is not, because objectives, constraints, alternatives, horizon, and capacity to absorb loss are properties of the participant rather than of the market.

Decision quality is a property of the process, and it has to be evaluated separately from the outcome — which means it cannot be evaluated one decision at a time. Uncertainty should change how much you commit, how quickly, and how reversibly, rather than only how you describe the choice. Confidence, the margin between alternatives, and the size of the commitment are three different things. The status quo is a decision. And the reasoning is worth writing down, because memory reliably preserves the outcome and discards the uncertainty.

This is where the framework stops. It can tell you what the evidence supports and how confident you are entitled to be. It cannot tell you what to do, and any version of it that claims otherwise has stopped being the framework.

Conclusion — From Market Understanding to Market Practice

The question this book was actually about

Eleven chapters ago this book started with two markets receiving the same news and producing different outcomes. It has spent the intervening pages building vocabulary: capacity, exposure, variability, direction, configuration, state, transition, decision environment.

None of that vocabulary will help you predict a market. What it does is let you answer a different question, and one you will face constantly:

How do you tell whether a claim about markets deserves your trust?

You will be shown claims for the rest of your life. Research findings. Backtests. Models. Dashboards. Explanations of yesterday's move, generated in seconds by systems that have never been wrong about anything in a way you could detect. Some of it will be excellent. Most of it will be confident, fluent, and unfalsifiable.

This closing chapter is about that. It is also about what this framework does not establish, which is a longer list than you might expect, and the most important thing in it.

What the framework establishes

Set out plainly, so that it can be measured against what follows.

It treats markets as evolving systems shaped by interaction, feedback, adaptation, heterogeneity, and nonlinear response. It organizes observation around four foundational domains — liquidity, positioning, volatility, and trend — while recognizing that these interact and do not exhaust what determines market behavior. It separates observation, measurement, evidence, inference, interpretation, assessment, judgment, and decision, and requires uncertainty, missingness, model dependence, and claim strength to stay visible. And it provides structures for making complex work traceable: market configuration, state representation, transition analysis, and the Decision Environment.

That is a vocabulary and a set of methodological boundaries. It is not a theory of what markets will do.

What it does not establish

This is the part that matters most, and it is the part that would disappear first if this book were shortened by someone in a hurry.

Volume I of the underlying work does not establish a complete theory of financial markets. It does not establish a final taxonomy of domains — the four are foundational, not settled, and the case for a fifth built around funding and collateral is open. It does not establish universal state categories, or universal thresholds. It does not establish a causal hierarchy among market forces. **It does not establish a forecasting advantage of any kind.** It does not establish one correct decision method. And it does not claim that latent constructs like positioning, fragility, or market state can be observed without modeling assumptions, because they cannot.

Nor does it establish that multidomain analysis will outperform simpler approaches. Some questions are answered adequately by one measurement, one domain, or one carefully specified statistical relationship. **The framework earns its place only when the added structure improves understanding, measurement, or decision quality enough to justify its complexity** — and whether it does is an open empirical question rather than a demonstrated result.

Stating this is not modesty and it is not a legal disclaimer. It is the condition under which anything else in the book can be trusted. A framework that will not name its own limits has no way of telling you when it is failing, and a framework that cannot fail cannot be evaluated.

Judging a claim

Claims about markets come in types, and the evidence required rises steeply with the type. This is the single most portable idea in this chapter.

Claim	The question it answers	What it minimally requires
Descriptive	What occurred?	Valid observation, coverage, measurement, uncertainty
Associative	What varies together?	Comparison, dependence analysis, consideration of confounds
Predictive	Does this improve estimates of a future outcome?	Out-of-sample design, a baseline, leakage controls, calibration
Causal	Would changing one thing alter another?	Identification assumptions, a counterfactual design, sensitivity

The strength of the evidence must be proportional to the strength of the claim. Temporal sequence does not establish causation. Predictive accuracy does not establish mechanism. And a claim stated at one level while supported at another is the most common failure you will encounter, precisely because the sentence looks the same either way.

Two further questions are worth asking of any claim.

What would weaken it? A claim that explains every possible outcome cannot be tested and is functioning as a belief. A useful claim identifies observations that would narrow it, weaken it, or force it to be restated.

How broad is it? **A conclusion cannot cover a wider population than the design represented.** A finding from large-capitalization US equities during regular trading hours, using one data vendor and one classification method over one volatility regime, does not automatically transport to other instruments, sessions, countries, or conditions. When transport fails, the correct response is to narrow the claim rather than to force it wider.

Judging research

A few of the ways research goes wrong are worth recognizing on sight.

Exploration presented as confirmation. Exploratory work — searching for patterns, testing variables, trying transformations — is essential and creates selection risk, because researchers see many possibilities and remember the compelling ones. Confirmatory work evaluates a specified hypothesis under a design fixed in advance. Treating the two as one activity inflates confidence dramatically, and the resulting claim looks identical to a genuine finding.

Multiple testing. Testing many variables, thresholds, horizons, transformations, and subgroups raises the chance that the surviving result reflects the search rather than the market. No single correction removes this entirely.

Overfitting. A model that captures noise or sample-specific structure rather than a repeatable relationship. Warning signs: excessive complexity, unstable parameters, strong in-sample and weak out-of-sample results, sensitivity to small sample changes, and performance concentrated in one unusual period.

Row count mistaken for information. Market observations are rarely independent. Dependence arises from time series, overlapping windows, common events, index membership, and cross-sectional correlation. **A dataset's number of rows can substantially exceed its effective information**, which means an impressive-sounding sample size may support far less than it appears to.

Assumed stability. Relevant properties of markets change: means, variances, correlations, tail behavior, participant composition, microstructure, policy, and the measurement process itself. **Relationships should be assumed capable of changing unless stability has been demonstrated.** A model spanning a structural break without acknowledging it may produce an average that describes no actual period.

Statistical significance mistaken for importance. Significance is evidence relative to a statistical model and a null hypothesis. It is not economic importance, causal validity, predictive stability, or usefulness for a decision. A small effect can be statistically significant in a very large sample and operationally irrelevant.

Outliers deleted. Automatic removal of extreme observations can eliminate exactly the episodes that would reveal how a market behaves under stress — which is frequently the question that mattered.

Publication survival. Published results skew toward the significant, the novel, and the narratively clean. **Publication status and evidentiary**

status are not the same thing, and null results and failed replications belong in the record rather than in a drawer.

Judging a backtest

Backtests deserve their own treatment, because they are the most persuasive artifact in retail finance and the easiest to construct dishonestly without intending to.

A backtest is a historical simulation under declared assumptions. It is not a live experiment, not proof of future profitability, and not a substitute for a plausible mechanism. Five questions cover most of what can go wrong.

Was every input actually available at the simulated decision time? Revised economic data, finalized index membership, complete option chains that did not exist in real time, and retrospectively assigned labels all produce impressive and impossible results.

Could the assumed trades have been filled, at those prices, in that size? Depth, urgency, and side all matter, and a simulation that assumes execution at the midpoint has assumed away the domain of Chapter 4.

Are the costs in there? Spread, fees, slippage, market impact, borrowing costs, funding, and tax. **These can dominate a small statistical edge entirely**, and their omission is the most common single defect.

How much capital can this actually absorb? A method may work at small scale and change its own execution conditions at larger scale.

Were the parameters chosen without contaminating the test? Repeatedly consulting a test set converts it into another tuning set, and the independence that made it meaningful is gone.

There is a case worth remembering as a template. A signal appears predictive in sample and fails out of sample. Review reveals that many thresholds were tested, the best was selected retrospectively, transaction costs were omitted, the test period overlapped the tuning period, and performance depended on one unusual episode.

The correct disposition is not "it doesn't work." It is: **unsupported as a stable predictive finding, retained as exploratory evidence, and preserved as a case study in selection bias** — so that the next person does not unknowingly repeat the same search.

Judging a model

Chapter 3 introduced what a model is. A few additions complete the picture.

Complexity has to earn its place. Every model should be compared against credible simple alternatives: naive persistence, a historical average, a simple threshold, an existing method, or governed human judgment. A complex model evaluated only against no model has not been evaluated.

Correct code is not a correct model. Verification asks whether an implementation matches its specification. Validation asks whether the specification was appropriate. A model can pass the first and fail the second completely.

Calibration and discrimination are different questions. A model may rank cases well while assigning inaccurate probabilities, or be well calibrated overall while ranking poorly.

Someone else's model is still your responsibility. External provenance changes what can be inspected; it does not transfer accountability. A supplier's documentation, benchmarks, or client list are evidence about the product, not a substitute for evaluating whether it fits your purpose, your data, and your situation. And where a supplied model has been customized, recalibrated, or wrapped in overlays, the deployed system is materially different from the one that was evaluated. Limited visibility into proprietary internals raises rather than lowers the importance of monitoring, benchmarking, and documented limitations.

Optimization can solve the wrong problem. An optimizer finds the best solution to the problem as specified. Whether that was the right problem is a separate question it cannot ask.

Models decay. Participants adapt, market structure changes, data sources change, strategies become crowded. Stable historical performance is evidence, not an entitlement. And a model can be applied outside the context it was approved for, which is a distinct failure from the model being wrong.

Retirement is a functioning outcome, not an admission. A model whose assumptions no longer hold, whose data are unavailable, or whose replacement is better should be retired — and retired does not mean erased. The historical versions, rationale, and known failures remain valuable.

Judging an explanation you did not write

This has become urgent recently, and the framework handles it well.

Suppose an automated system produces a persuasive explanation for a sharp market decline. It attributes the move to crowded positioning, dealer hedging, weakening liquidity, and rising uncertainty. The narrative is coherent, the mechanism is plausible, and the prose is better than most human commentary.

Coherence is not evidence. Ask:

Which sources were used? Were the observations current? Which statements are measurements and which are inferences? Are the ownership assumptions behind the dealer claim valid, or assumed? Has the trigger been distinguished from the structural condition? Were alternative hypotheses considered? Is uncertainty preserved anywhere in it? And can the narrative be reproduced from the evidence it cites?

If the explanation cannot answer those questions, it remains an unverified narrative regardless of how fluent it is. Automated systems can fabricate evidence, produce plausible but unsupported causal accounts, obscure where their claims came from, and drift between versions. Fluency is not evidence, and an explanation that sounds coherent is not scientifically stronger unless its observations, measurements, claims, and sources can be traced and challenged.

The useful framing is that the unit to evaluate is not the machine and not the person, but the complete arrangement: the data, the models, the interfaces, the authority boundaries, the incentives, the controls, and the review process. Machines are strong at scale, consistency, and structured search. Humans remain responsible for objectives, context, ethical boundaries, challenge, and accountability. **Provenance, validation, and responsibility cannot be delegated to fluency.**

Why things stop working

One theme has appeared in every chapter and deserves consolidating.

Participants respond to prices, to forecasts, to published research, to model outputs, and to each other. Once a relationship becomes widely used, it may weaken, reverse, migrate to a different horizon, or change the execution conditions around it. Widely followed thresholds alter behavior at those thresholds. Widespread use of similar rules makes responses correlated.

A deployed model may become part of the system it is trying to represent. A successful method can weaken its own future performance by changing what participants do.

This is not a reason for despair, and it is a reason that market knowledge decays in a way that knowledge in most other fields does not. Decay should be expected and monitored rather than treated as a surprise when it arrives.

An open program, and how to tell if it is failing

The framework in this book is presented as an open research program rather than a finished doctrine. That phrase is easy to say and worth making concrete.

Openness here is primarily about evidence, not disclosure. It does not require that every dataset, algorithm, or proprietary implementation be published — data licenses, confidentiality, security, and competitive constraints are real. What it requires is that **the standing of a claim must not depend solely on institutional authority**. Where public replication is impossible, internal reproducibility, independent audit, controlled external review, or replication under agreement can still do the work.

Progress in such a program means clearer definitions, stronger measurement validity, better reproducibility, more stable classification, improved calibration, fewer false transitions, more informative uncertainty, and more disciplined decision records. It emphatically does not mean more terminology or more models. **Narrowing or retiring a claim is progress** — if a broad relationship fails outside one period but survives under specific conditions, the narrower statement is scientifically stronger even though it sounds less impressive.

And a program should be able to recognize its own failure. The signs: definitions that cannot be applied consistently; measurements that cannot be reproduced; model outputs that add nothing over simple baselines; transition systems that are chronically too noisy or too late; classifications that drift away from observable evidence. Institutional failure looks different: negative findings disappearing, conflicts going undisclosed, commercial incentives determining scientific conclusions, models retained after their assumptions fail, and language becoming so flexible that no observation could ever count against it.

A framework that names its own failure conditions is offering you something. A framework that does not is asking you to take its word.

What would change the four

It is worth making the revisability of the four domains concrete, because a framework that says it is open to revision without describing what revision would look like has said nothing.

Suppose repeated studies across several markets showed that funding and collateral conditions explain important variation in how stress transmits — variation that cannot be represented adequately within the existing four categories. That is not a hypothetical objection; it is the most commonly raised gap, and the scholarly volume names it as an open question rather than answering it.

Several responses would be available. Funding could be treated as a sub-part of liquidity. It could be represented as a condition that cuts across all four domains. The domain definitions could be revised. A fifth domain could be added. Or the scope of the four-domain architecture could be narrowed to the contexts where it works.

The important part is how such a decision should be made. **No answer should be selected because it preserves the simplicity of the existing structure.** The choice should follow the evidence, the conceptual clarity of each option, the validity of the available measurements, and whether the result replicates. The four domains are foundational. They are not immune to the evidence generated within them, and a version of this framework that treated them as settled would have stopped being a research program.

Two things about who is telling you this

The framework described in this book was developed at the WallStreet-Delta Institute, which is also its steward, its publisher, and the builder of tools that operationalize it. That is a conflict, and it is better named than managed quietly.

Credibility under those conditions requires external review, independent replication, disclosure of conflicts, documented dissent, correction mechanisms, and separation of research approval from commercial incentives where practical. **A research program becomes stronger when its claims can survive competent review outside the institution that introduced them**, and that review has not yet happened at scale.

There is a related discipline that applies directly to how anything built on this framework may be sold. Four claim layers must stay distinct: what the **research** supports, what a validated **model** can represent, what a deployed **product** actually delivers, and what **marketing** communicates. **No product or marketing claim should be stronger than the research, validation, and implementation evidence beneath it.** Applied to this book: nothing here claims that using this framework improves investment returns, because no evidence establishing that exists.

The second thing is about originality. Almost nothing in these pages is new. Liquidity, positioning, volatility, and trend are deeply established fields with extensive literatures. So are measurement theory, causal inference, decision theory, model risk management, reproducible research, and the philosophy of science that the epistemic chapters rest on. The framework does not claim to have originated the distinction between observation and theory, provisional knowledge, hypothesis testing, model uncertainty, Bayesian updating, replication, or decision analysis.

What is proposed here is organization, not discovery: the arrangement of established disciplines into one architecture for market reasoning that starts with observation rather than with an indicator, and preserves the path from measurement to evidence to assessment to judgment to decision. Saying so is accuracy, not humility, and a framework that overstated its originality would have failed its own standards in the first chapter.

What to do with this

The framework does not tell you what to buy, and that limitation is not a gap to be filled by a subsequent volume. It follows from the framework's own content: if the same evidence rationally supports different actions for participants with different objectives, constraints, and capacity, then no analysis can produce a universal instruction. Anything claiming to has abandoned the argument.

What it can change is more modest and more durable. You can now ask of any market claim: what type of claim is this, and is the evidence proportional to it? What was measured, over what horizon, by what method, against what baseline? Is this an observation or a model output? What alternative explanations were considered, and what would have distinguished them? What is the confidence, and confidence in *what* exactly? What would change this assessment?

Those questions are unglamorous and they are extraordinarily effective. Most market commentary cannot survive three of them. Some of it survives all six, and learning to tell the difference is worth more than any indicator.

A closing perspective

Markets will keep changing faster than any fixed framework can capture. New instruments, regulations, technologies, participant behaviors, and institutional structures will alter both what happens and what can be measured about it. The task is not to eliminate uncertainty or freeze market behavior into permanent categories.

The task is to improve how market phenomena are observed, measured, interpreted, challenged, represented, and revised. To make uncertainty more visible rather than hiding it. To make models more accountable rather than more authoritative. To make decisions more reviewable rather than merely more automated.

A discipline organized this way should ultimately be judged not by whether it predicts correctly, but by whether it produces clearer questions, more trustworthy measurements, more defensible claims, more transparent models, more responsible decisions, and a greater capacity to learn from error.

That is a slower standard than the one most market content is measured against. It has the advantage of being achievable, and of being the only kind of progress that accumulates.

The final commitment, which applies to this book as much as to anything it describes: **correction over consistency, refinement over institutional pride, and cumulative learning over any claim of final certainty.**

Glossary

Terms used in this book, in the sense the scholarly volume gives them. This list is shorter than the canonical glossary and does not replace it: where a fuller or narrower technical meaning matters, *Foundations of Market Systems Science*, Volume I, Appendix A governs. No term is defined here in a way that departs from it.

Assessment — A structured synthesis of evidence, alternatives, contradictions, uncertainty, and confidence, for a stated analytical purpose. Distinct from the judgment or decision that may follow.

Breadth — How widely market movement or participation is distributed across a defined universe, rather than concentrated in a small subset.

Configuration — The detailed, time-specific arrangement of observed and inferred conditions across domains and other relevant evidence, at a stated scale. A configuration preserves detail; a state compresses it.

Configuration dependence — That the effect of information, order flow, or a disturbance depends on the market configuration in which it occurs.

Confidence — The strength of support for a specific claim or output. Confidence is multidimensional and is not a property of an analysis as a whole. It is also not the same thing as probability.

Crowding — Similarity of exposures, assumptions, or response rules across participants. Distinct from concentration, which concerns how exposure is distributed rather than how alike it is.

Decision — Selection among available alternatives within a Decision Environment.

Decision Environment — The structured combination of objectives, constraints, alternatives, information, uncertainty, horizon, risk capacity, implementation conditions, reversibility, authority, and responsibility relevant to a particular choice.

Decision margin — An Institute term for the degree by which a preferred alternative exceeds the next-best alternative under stated assumptions and objectives. A transparent analytical device rather than established general usage.

Decision quality — The quality of the process used to choose an action under uncertainty, evaluated separately from whether the realized outcome was favorable.

Decomposable — Able to be traced back from a compressed output to its component measurements, assumptions, transformations, quality states, and confidence. A composite that cannot be decomposed is not a summary of evidence.

Domain (observational domain) — A conceptual category used to organize evidence about one dimension of market behavior. This book uses liquidity, positioning, volatility, and trend. A domain is not a measurement, an indicator, a causal force, or a predictive model.

Evidence — A measurement or observation evaluated as relevant to a particular question, proposition, comparison, or hypothesis. A measurement becomes evidence only in relation to a question.

Fast trajectory — A short-horizon description of recent multidomain movement, relative to a confirmed structural state. Trajectory is not confirmation.

Fragility — Sensitivity to disturbance, amplification, constraint activation, or loss of function, under specified conditions. Inferred rather than directly observed.

Hysteresis — A design device that reduces unstable switching near a boundary by requiring different evidence to enter a classification than to leave it, or by requiring persistence before reclassification. It improves stability and introduces lag.

Implied volatility — The volatility input that reconciles an option-pricing model with an observed option price, given the other inputs and assumptions. It is model-conditioned and is not a pure or unbiased forecast of future realized volatility.

Inference — A proposition that extends beyond direct observation or measurement, through reasoning and assumptions.

Judgment — A reasoned conclusion formed for a stated purpose. Distinct from the participant-specific decision that may follow.

Liquidity — A market's capacity for exchange under specified size, horizon, venue, side, urgency, and market conditions. Multidimensional rather than a single quantity, and not synonymous with volume.

Market Compass — An Institute presentation model for communicating selected multidomain state components while preserving decomposition, freshness, and confidence. It is not the market state itself.

Market state — A controlled, higher-level representation of selected features of a market configuration, for a stated purpose, horizon, universe, and method. Assigned by an analyst or model rather than possessed by the market.

Measurement — A controlled representation constructed from data according to a defined method and purpose. A measurement represents an aspect of a phenomenon without being that phenomenon.

Missingness — The state in which potentially relevant evidence is unavailable, absent, invalid, delayed, or structurally unobservable. Missingness is not equivalent to neutrality.

Model — A simplified, purpose-specific representation of selected features, relationships, or processes within a defined system. Every model selects, imposes structure, and omits.

Perspective — The plain-English word used in this book for an observational domain: one of the four ways of looking at a market. See **Domain**, which is the term the framework uses. A perspective belongs to the observer, not to the market, and no one of them is sufficient on its own.

Positioning — The distribution of exposure, sensitivity, leverage, concentration, and potential adjustment requirements across participants or instruments, much of which may be latent, delayed, or model-dependent.

Provisional knowledge — The principle that market understanding is the current best-supported account permitted by available evidence, measurements, models, assumptions, and scope, and remains open to revision. It does not mean that all interpretations are equally valid, or that conclusions should be withheld.

Realized volatility — Variability estimated from observed price changes over a defined interval and sampling scheme. Its value is inseparable from its method of construction.

Recorded observation — A value or event reported by an identified source under a specified timestamp, schema, and context. It establishes what the source reported, not the complete meaning or cause of what occurred.

Resilience — The capacity to absorb disturbance, continue functioning, replenish, adapt, or recover, under specified conditions.

Risk capacity — The ability to absorb adverse outcomes without violating essential objectives or obligations. Distinct from risk tolerance, which is willingness rather than ability.

Scenario — A conditional pathway describing how events or configurations may evolve under stated assumptions and signposts. A scenario is not a forecast.

Signal — A rule-generated indication intended to inform a decision. Distinct from a state, a forecast, and a universal instruction.

Structural State Vector — An Institute decomposable representation of selected domain and cross-domain state variables at a defined time and horizon. A governed representation of selected evidence, not a self-validating description of the market.

Threshold — A designed boundary used to convert continuous variation into a category, alert, decision rule, or state change. Thresholds are design choices, not natural boundaries.

Trajectory — The direction and pattern of recent change in selected configuration components.

Transition — A material and sufficiently persistent reorganization of selected configuration features, under a stated method, horizon, and classification framework. All confirmed transitions involve configuration change; most configuration changes do not become confirmed transitions.

Trend — Sustained directional persistence in a market variable, over a specified horizon, identified through a stated measurement method. Not an independent causal force and not a forecast.

Uncertainty — Incomplete confidence about a claim, outcome, model, measurement, or future condition. Distinct from missing information, measurement uncertainty, model uncertainty, and error — the last of which should be corrected rather than reclassified as uncertainty.

Volatility — The degree and structure of variability observed or implied in market prices, over a specified horizon and method. One expression of uncertainty, sensitivity, information processing, and adjustment — not uncertainty itself, and not risk, fear, instability, or direction.

Further Reading

Start here

Foundations of Market Systems Science*, Volume I — *Understanding, Evolution, and Decision in Financial Markets. Saeed Mohammad, WallStreetDelta Institute.

This book is a retail edition drawn from that volume. Volume I is roughly twice the length and carries what this edition deliberately leaves out: the full argument, the measurement and research standards, the model-governance architecture, the sixty-seven-principle register, ten appendices, and the complete bibliography from which the selection below is drawn.

If any distinction in this book mattered to you and you want it developed properly, that is where it is developed. Where the two differ in meaning, the scholarly volume governs.

A short selection of prior work

The framework's contribution is organization rather than discovery, and the disciplines it organizes are established and prior. The following is a small sample of that literature, grouped by the chapters they bear on. It is not a reading list for the framework; it is a set of doors out of it.

On how markets are studied as systems. Ludwig von Bertalanffy, *General System Theory* (1968). John H. Holland, *Hidden Order: How Adaptation Builds Complexity* (1995). Melanie Mitchell, *Complexity: A Guided Tour* (2009). W. Brian Arthur, *Complexity and the Economy* (2015).

On evidence, inference, and what research can establish. Karl R. Popper, *The Logic of Scientific Discovery* (1959). Thomas S. Kuhn, *The Structure of Scientific Revolutions* (1962). George E. P. Box, "Science and Statistics" (1976). John P. A. Ioannidis, "Why Most Published Research Findings Are False" (2005).

On liquidity and market structure. Albert S. Kyle, "Continuous Auctions and Insider Trading" (1985). Lawrence R. Glosten and Paul

R. Milgrom, "Bid, Ask and Transaction Prices" (1985). Maureen O'Hara, *Market Microstructure Theory* (1995). Joel Hasbrouck, *Empirical Market Microstructure* (2007). Markus K. Brunnermeier and Lasse Heje Pedersen, "Market Liquidity and Funding Liquidity" (2009).

On volatility. Benoit B. Mandelbrot, "The Variation of Certain Speculative Prices" (1963). Robert F. Engle's 1982 paper introducing ARCH, and Tim Bollerslev's 1986 extension to GARCH. Nassim Nicholas Taleb, *Dynamic Hedging* (1997).

On direction, efficiency, and adaptation. Eugene F. Fama, "Efficient Capital Markets" (1970). Robert J. Shiller on stock prices and dividends (1981). Andrew W. Lo, "The Adaptive Markets Hypothesis" (2004).

On deciding under uncertainty. Frank H. Knight, *Risk, Uncertainty and Profit* (1921). John von Neumann and Oskar Morgenstern, *Theory of Games and Economic Behavior* (1944). Leonard J. Savage, *The Foundations of Statistics* (1954). Daniel Kahneman and Amos Tversky, "Prospect Theory" (1979). Ronald A. Howard and James E. Matheson, *Readings on the Principles and Applications of Decision Analysis* (1989).

On models, and on what goes wrong with them. Leo Breiman, "Statistical Modeling: The Two Cultures" (2001). Judea Pearl, *Causality* (2009). Campbell R. Harvey, Yan Liu, and Heqing Zhu on the cross-section of expected returns (2016). Christoph Molnar, *Interpretable Machine Learning* (2022). And, for how institutions are expected to govern models, the Federal Reserve and OCC *Supervisory Guidance on Model Risk Management* (2011).

A note on this list

It is deliberately short and deliberately incomplete. Volume I's bibliography runs to fifty-three verified entries and its Appendix J carries a fuller suggested-reading treatment. Nothing here is a recommendation about markets, and inclusion does not imply that the framework agrees with a work — several of the above disagree sharply with one another, which is part of why they are worth reading.

Index

www.ingramcontent.com/pod-product-compliance
Lightning Source LLC
LaVergne TN
LVHW010722061126
851857LV00014B/1308